Important Instruction

Students, Parents, and Teachers can use the URL or QR code provided below to access two full-length Lumos GMAS practice tests. Please note that these assessments are provided in the Online format only.

URL	QR Code
Visit the URL below and place the book access code **http://www.lumoslearning.com/a/tedbooks** **Access Code: GMASMG3-94203-S**	

lumos learning
Developed by Expert Teachers

GMAS Online Assessments and 3rd Grade Math Practice Workbook, Student Copy

Contributing Editor	-	**Keyana M. Martinez**
Contributing Editor	-	**LaSina McLain-Jackson**
Contributing Editor	-	**Greg Applegate**
Executive Producer	-	**Mukunda Krishnaswamy**
Designer and Illustrator	-	**Sowmya R.**

First Edition - 2020

NGA Center/CCSSO are the sole owners and developers of the Common Core State Standards, which does not sponsor or endorse this product. © Copyright 2010. National Governors Association Center for Best Practices and Council of Chief State School Officers.

Georgia Department of Education is not affiliated to Lumos Learning. Georgia Department of Education, was not involved in the production of, and does not endorse these products or this site.

ISBN-10: 1542666554

ISBN-13: 978-1542666558

Printed in the United States of America

For permissions and additional information contact us

Lumos Information Services, LLC
PO Box 1575, Piscataway, NJ 08855-1575
http://www.LumosLearning.com

Email: support@lumoslearning.com
Tel: (732) 384-0146
Fax: (866) 283-6471

Developed by Expert Teachers

INTRODUCTION

About Lumos tedBook for GMAS Test Practice:
This book is specifically designed to improve student achievement on the GMAS. Students perform at their best on standardized tests when they feel comfortable with the test content as well as the test format. Lumos tedBook for GMAS test ensures this with meticulously designed practice that adheres to the guidelines provided by the GMAS for the number of questions, standards, difficulty level, sessions, question types, and duration.

About Lumos Smart Test Prep:
With more than a decade of experience and expertise in developing practice resources for standardized tests, Lumos Learning has developed the most efficient methodology to help students succeed on the state assessments (See Figure 1).

Lumos Smart Test Prep Methodology offers students realistic GMAS assessment rehearsal along with providing an efficient pathway to overcome each proficiency gap.

The process starts with students taking the online diagnostic assessment. This online diagnostic test will help assess students' proficiency levels in various standards. With the completion of this diagnostic assessment, Lumos generates a personalized study plan with a standard checklist based on student performance in the online diagnostic test. Parents and educators can use this study plan to remediate the proficiency gaps with targeted standards-based practice available in the workbook.

After student completes the targeted remedial practice, they should attempt the second online GMAS practice test. Upon finishing the second assessment, Lumos will generate another individualized study plan by identifying topics that require more practice. Based on these practice suggestions, further skill building activities can be planned to help students gain comprehensive mastery needed to ensure success on the state assessment.

Lumos Smart Test Prep Methodology

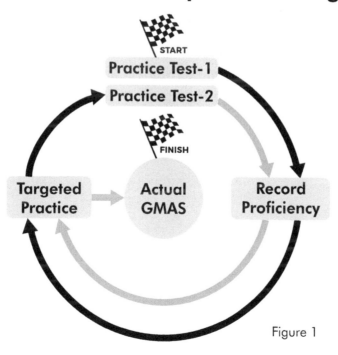

Figure 1

Table of Contents

Sign Up Online

GMAS

Grade 3 Math Practice

Unlock Digital Access

2 GMAS Practice Tests

3 Math Domains

Sign Up Now

Url: https://LumosLearning/a/tedbooks

Access Code: GMASMG3-94203-S

Access GMAS Test
Practice Resources
On Your Mobile Device

Online Access

for

GMAS Practice

Printed Workbook

for

Skills Practice

Download Lumos StepUp App
from Google Play Store or Apple App Store

After installing the StepUp App, scan this **QR Code** via **tedBook** section of the mobile app

Chapter 1

Lumos Smart Test Prep Methodology

Step 1: Access Online GMAS Practice Test

The online GMAS practice tests mirror the actual Georgia Milestones Assessment System (GMAS) in the number of questions, item types, test duration, test tools, and more.

After completing the test, your student will receive immediate feedback with detailed reports on standards mastery and a personalized study plan to overcome any learning gaps. With this study plan, use the next section of the workbook to practice.

Use the URL and access code provided below or scan the QR code to access the first GMAS practice test to get started.

URL	QR Code
Visit the URL below and place the book access code **http://www.lumoslearning.com/a/tedbooks** **Access Code: GMASMG3-94203-S**	

Step 2: Review the Personalized Study Plan Online

After students complete the online Practice Test 1, they can access their individualized study plan from the table of contents (Figure 2) Parents and Teachers can also review the study plan through their Lumos account (parent or teacher) portal.

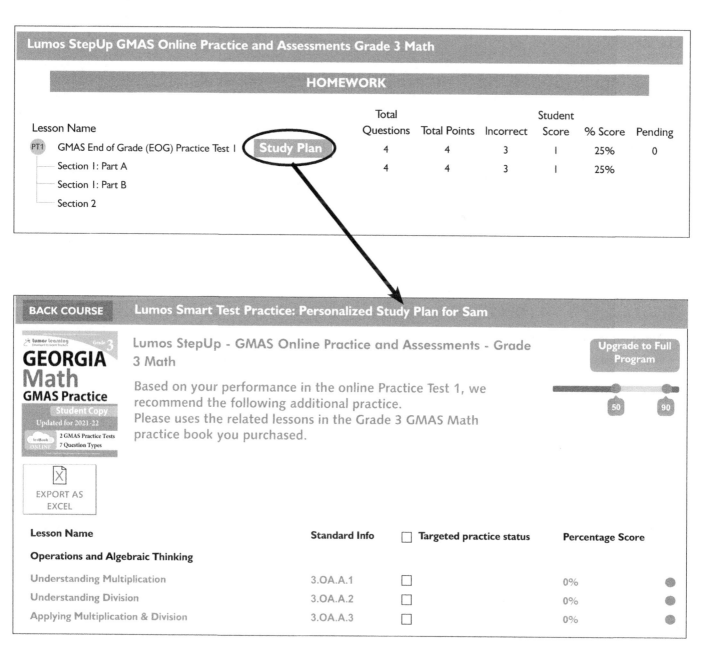

Figure 2

Step 3: Complete Targeted Practice

Using the information provided in the study plan report, complete the targeted practice using the appropriate lessons to overcome proficiency gaps. With lesson names included in the study plan, find the appropriate topics in this workbook and answer the questions provided. Marking the completed lessons in the study plan after each practice session is recommended.(See Figure 3)

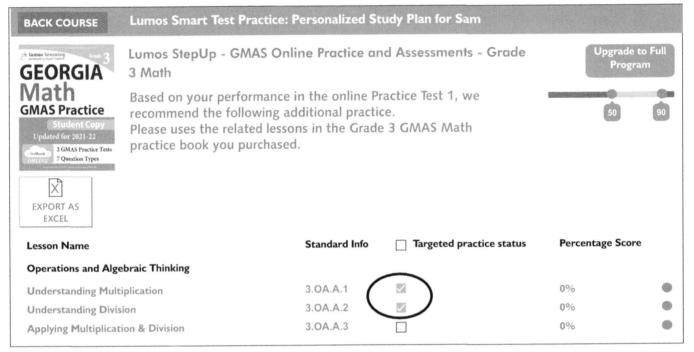

Figure 3

Step 4: Access the Practice Test 2 Online

After completing the targeted practice in this workbook, students should attempt the second GMAS practice test online. Using the student login name and password, login to the Lumos website to complete the second practice test.

Step 5: Repeat Targeted Practice

Repeat the targeted practice as per Step 3 using the second study plan report for Practice test 2 after completion of the second GMAS rehearsal.

Visit http://www.lumoslearning.com/a/lstp for more information on Lumos Smart Test Prep Methodology or Scan the QR Code

Test Taking Tips

1) **The day before the test,** make sure you get a good night's sleep.

2) **On the day of the test,** be sure to eat a good hearty breakfast! Also, be sure to arrive at school on time.

3) **During the test:**

- **Read each question carefully.**

  - Do not spend too much time on any one question. Work steadily through all questions in the section.
  - Attempt all the questions even if you are not sure of some answers.
  - If you run into a difficult question, eliminate as many choices as you can and then pick the best one from the remaining choices. Intelligent guessing will help you increase your score.
  - Also, mark the question so that if you have extra time, you can return to it after you reach the end of the section.
  - Some questions may refer to a graph, chart, or other kind of picture. Carefully review the infographics before answering the question.
  - Be sure to include explanations for your written responses and show all work.

- **While Answering Multiple-choice (EBSR) questions.**

  - Select the bubble corresponding to your answer choice.
  - Read all of the answer choices, even if think you have found the correct answer.

- **While Answering TECR questions.**

  - Read the directions of each question. Some might ask you to drag something, others to select, and still others to highlight. Follow all instructions of the question (or questions if it is in multiple parts)

Chapter 2:
Operations and Algebraic Thinking

Lesson 1: Understanding Multiplication

You can scan the QR code given below or use the url to access additional EdSearch resources including videos and mobile apps related to *Understanding Multiplication*.

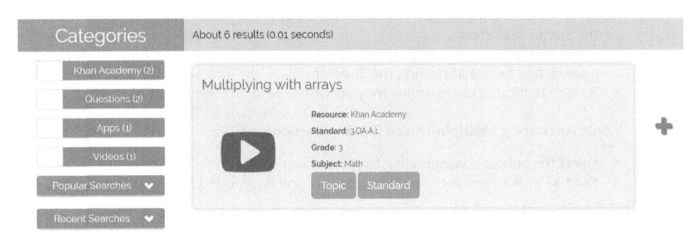

Categories	About 6 results (0.01 seconds)
Khan Academy (2)	**Multiplying with arrays**
Questions (2)	Resource: Khan Academy
Apps (1)	Standard: 3.OA.A.1
Videos (1)	Grade: 3
Popular Searches ⌄	Subject: Math
Recent Searches ⌄	Topic Standard

ed)Search   *Understanding Multiplication*

URL	QR Code
http://www.lumoslearning.com/a/3oaa1	

1. Which multiplication fact is being modeled below?

    Ⓐ 3 x 10 = 30
    Ⓑ 4 x 10 = 40
    Ⓒ 4 x 9 = 36
    Ⓓ 3 x 9 = 27

2. Which numerical expression describes this array?

    Ⓐ 4 + 5
    Ⓑ 5 + 4
    Ⓒ 4 x 5
    Ⓓ 4 x 4

3. Which number sentence describes this array?

    Ⓐ 8 x 4 = 32
    Ⓑ 7 + 5 = 12
    Ⓒ 5 x 7 = 35
    Ⓓ 4 x 7 = 28

4. Which number sentence describes this array?

    Ⓐ 2 x 12 = 24
    Ⓑ 2 + 12 = 14
    Ⓒ 12 + 2 = 24
    Ⓓ 10 x 2 = 20

5. Identify the multiplication sentence for the picture below:

Ⓐ 4 x 4 = 16
Ⓑ 4 x 3 = 12
Ⓒ 3 x 4 = 12
Ⓓ 4 x 2 = 8

6. What multiplication fact does this picture model?

○○○○○○
○○○○○○
○○○○○○
○○○○○○

Ⓐ 4 x 6 = 24
Ⓑ 4 x 7 = 28
Ⓒ 6 x 3 = 18
Ⓓ 7 x 4 = 28

7. Identify the multiplication sentence for the picture below:

Ⓐ 7 x 2 = 14
Ⓑ 7 x 3 = 21
Ⓒ 7 x 4 = 28
Ⓓ 6 x 3 = 18

8. Identify the multiplication sentence for the picture below:

Ⓐ 4 x 4 = 16
Ⓑ 3 x 6 = 18
Ⓒ 3 x 4 = 12
Ⓓ 3 x 5 = 15

9. Identify the multiplication sentence for the picture below:

Ⓐ 3 x 2 = 6
Ⓑ 3 x 3 = 9
Ⓒ 4 x 2 = 8
Ⓓ 3 x 1 = 3

10. Identify the multiplication sentence for the picture below:

Ⓐ 3 x 5 = 15
Ⓑ 4 x 4 = 16
Ⓒ 5 x 4 = 20
Ⓓ 7 x 4 = 28

11. Identify the multiplication sentence for the picture below:

Ⓐ 2 x 5 = 10
Ⓑ 4 x 2 = 8
Ⓒ 4 x 1 = 4
Ⓓ 4 + 2 = 6

12. Identify the multiplication sentence for the picture below:

ᔑᔑᔑᔑᔑᔑᔑᔑ
ᔑᔑᔑᔑᔑᔑᔑᔑ
ᔑᔑᔑᔑᔑᔑᔑᔑ
ᔑᔑᔑᔑᔑᔑᔑᔑ
ᔑᔑᔑᔑᔑᔑᔑᔑ
ᔑᔑᔑᔑᔑᔑᔑᔑ

   Ⓐ 6 x 7 = 42
   Ⓑ 6 x 8 = 48
   Ⓒ 8 x 9 = 72
   Ⓓ 8 x 8 = 64

13. Identify the multiplication sentence for the picture below:

   Ⓐ 10 x 1 = 10
   Ⓑ 9 x 2 = 18
   Ⓒ 2 x 10 = 20
   Ⓓ 5 x 4 = 20

14. Identify the multiplication sentence for the picture below:

Ⓐ 5 x 5 = 25
Ⓑ 4 x 4 = 16
Ⓒ 4 x 6 = 24
Ⓓ 5 x 4 = 20

15. Identify the multiplication sentence for the picture below

Ⓐ 3 x 1 = 3
Ⓑ 5 x 3 = 15
Ⓒ 3 x 2 = 6
Ⓓ 3 x 3 = 9

16. Represent the below equation as a multiplication expression. Write your answer in the box below.

8 + 8 + 8 + 8?

17. Match each multiplication statement to the correct addition statement by darkening the corresponding circles.

	Column A: 3+3+3+3+3+3	Column B: 3+3+3+3+3+3+3+3	Column C: 3+3+3
3 x 8	○	○	○
3 x 3	○	○	○
3 x 6	○	○	○

18. For each of the picture, write the correct mathematical expression in the box.

   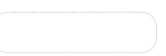

19. PART A

John finds the solution for 8 x 6 by solving for (8 x 5) + 8. Is John correct? Explain why you think that John's strategy is correct or not? Write your answer in the box below.

PART B

There are Seven boys, and each of them buys 6 pens. How many pens do they buy all together? Write an equation to represent this. Also, Find the total number of pens purchased using the equation.

20. Complete the following table:

Number of lions	5	6	9		
Total number of legs	20			32	16

Chapter 2

Lesson 2: Understanding Division

You can scan the QR code given below or use the url to access additional EdSearch resources including videos and mobile apps related to *Understanding Division*.

Understanding Division

URL	QR Code
http://www.lumoslearning.com/a/3oaa2	

1. George is canning pears. He has 100 pears and he divides the pears evenly among 10 pots. How many pears does George put in each pot?

   Ⓐ 9 pears
   Ⓑ 5 pears
   Ⓒ 8 pears
   Ⓓ 10 pears

2. Marisa made 15 woolen dolls. She gave the same number of woolen dolls to 3 friends. How many dolls did Marisa give to each friend?

   Ⓐ 4 woolen dolls
   Ⓑ 3 woolen dolls
   Ⓒ 5 woolen dolls
   Ⓓ 6 woolen dolls

3. Lisa bought 50 mangoes. She divided them equally into 5 basins. How many mangoes did Lisa put in each basin?

   Ⓐ 10 mangos
   Ⓑ 8 mangos
   Ⓒ 5 mangos
   Ⓓ 7 mangos

4. Jennifer picked 30 oranges from the basket. If it takes 6 oranges to make a one liter jar of juice, how many one liter jars of juice can Jennifer make?

   Ⓐ 4 jars
   Ⓑ 3 jars
   Ⓒ 6 jars
   Ⓓ 5 jars

5. Miller bought 80 rolls of paper towels. If there are 10 rolls of paper towels in each pack, how many packs of paper towels did Miller buy?

   Ⓐ 6 packs
   Ⓑ 8 packs
   Ⓒ 7 packs
   Ⓓ 5 packs

6. James takes 15 photographs of his school building. He gave the same number of photographs to 5 friends. How many photographs did James give to each friend?

Ⓐ 2 photographs
Ⓑ 3 photographs
Ⓒ 6 photographs
Ⓓ 5 photographs

7. Ron took 81 playing cards and arranged them into 9 equal piles. How many playing cards did Ron put in each pile?

Ⓐ 5 playing cards
Ⓑ 4 playing cards
Ⓒ 6 playing cards
Ⓓ 9 playing cards

8. Robert wants to buy 40 ice cream cups from the ice cream parlor. If there are 10 ice cream cups in each box, how many boxes of ice cream cups should Robert buy?

Ⓐ 6 boxes
Ⓑ 3 boxes
Ⓒ 4 boxes
Ⓓ 5 boxes

9. Marilyn wants to purchase 20 tiles. If the tiles come in packs of 5, how many packs should Marilyn buy?

Ⓐ 3 packs
Ⓑ 4 packs
Ⓒ 5 packs
Ⓓ 6 packs

10. There are 30 people running around the path. If the runners are evenly divided among the path's 5 lanes, how many people are running in each lane?

Ⓐ 6 runners
Ⓑ 5 runners
Ⓒ 8 runners
Ⓓ 4 runners

11. Sally is buying goodie bags for her class. She needs 24 bags in all. If the bags come in packs of 3, how many packs does Sally need?

Ⓐ 21 packs
Ⓑ 3 packs
Ⓒ 24 packs
Ⓓ 8 packs

12. Mr. Johnson is planting a garden. He wants to use all of his 44 seeds and wants to make 4 rows of vegetables. How many seeds should he plant in each row?

Ⓐ 22 seeds
Ⓑ 11 seeds
Ⓒ 4 seeds
Ⓓ 88 seeds

13. Destiny, Jimmy, and Marcy have 32 marbles all together. Tommy adds 4 marbles to the set. If the group of friends wants to evenly divide the marbles so that each person has the same number, how many marbles should each person receive?

Ⓐ 4 marbles
Ⓑ 8 marbles
Ⓒ 9 marbles
Ⓓ 10 marbles

14. Mr. Baker earned $100 for five days of work. If he made the same amount each day, how much money did he make per day?

Ⓐ $15 per day
Ⓑ $20 per day
Ⓒ $25 per day
Ⓓ $30 per day

15. Seth and his brother have collected 26 seashells on the beach. If they want to share them equally, how many seashells will each of them receive?

Ⓐ 6 seashells
Ⓑ 9 seashells
Ⓒ 26 seashells
Ⓓ 13 seashells

Name _____   Date _____

16. A pizza is cut into 8 slices. Tim and Kira want to share the pizza. If they both eat the same number of slices, how many slices will each person eat? Write it in the box given below.

17. Gabriela has 16 stickers. She wants to find two ways to divide the stickers into equal groups. Which expressions can she use to divide the stickers? Mark all the correct answers.

Ⓐ 16 ÷ 2
Ⓑ 16 ÷ 3
Ⓒ 16 ÷ 4
Ⓓ 16 ÷ 5

18. Circle the picture that shows the expression 10 ÷ 5.

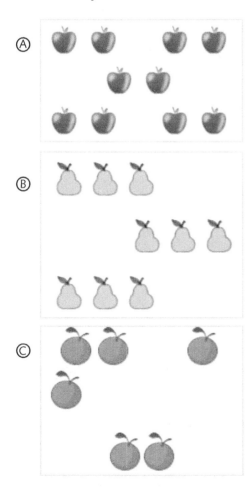

19. Miriam has 100 marbles. She wants to divide the marbles into equal groups. How many ways can she do this? Complete the table by listing all the possible ways in which you can divide 100. Write the missing numbers and fill the table. Enter the numbers in ascending order.

Dividend	Possible Divisors
100	2
100	4
100	
100	
100	20
100	25
100	

20. For each expression below, choose the correct symbol to be filled in the blank.

	<	>	=
30 ÷ 5 ____ 42 ÷ 6	○	○	○
72 ÷ 8 ____ 63 ÷ 7	○	○	○
54 ÷ 6 ____ 56 ÷ 7	○	○	○

Name _____   Date _____

Lesson 3: Applying Multiplication & Division

You can scan the QR code given below or use the url to access additional EdSearch resources including videos and mobile apps related to *Applying Multiplication & Division*.

Applying Multiplication & Division

URL	QR Code
http://www.lumoslearning.com/a/3oaa3	

1. **54 x 3 = ?**
    The product in this number sentence is _____.

    Ⓐ **54**
    Ⓑ **162**
    Ⓒ **3**
    Ⓓ **54 and 3**

2. **A Snack Shop has twice as many popcorn balls as they do cotton candy. If there are 30 popcorn balls, how many cotton candies are there?**

    Ⓐ **7**
    Ⓑ **450**
    Ⓒ **30**
    Ⓓ **15**

3. **Monica has 56 DVDs in her movie collection. This is 8 times as many as Sue has. How many DVDs does Sue have?**

    Ⓐ **8**
    Ⓑ **6**
    Ⓒ **7**
    Ⓓ **10**

4. **Jonathan can do 7 jumping jacks. Marcus can do 4 times as many as Jonathan. How many jumping jacks can Marcus do?**

    Ⓐ **28**
    Ⓑ **8**
    Ⓒ **4**
    Ⓓ **7**

5. **Darren has seen 4 movies this year. Marsha has seen 3 times as many movies as Darren. How many movies has Marsha seen?**

    Ⓐ **7**
    Ⓑ **3**
    Ⓒ **4**
    Ⓓ **12**

6. Sarah is planting a garden. She will plant 4 rows with 9 seeds in each row. How many plants will be in the garden?

  Ⓐ 32 plants
  Ⓑ 36 plants
  Ⓒ 42 plants
  Ⓓ 13 plants

7. Mrs. Huerta's class is having a pizza party. There are 24 students in the class. Each pizza has 12 slices. How many pizzas does Mrs. Huerta need to order for each child to have 1 slice?

  Ⓐ 3 pizzas
  Ⓑ 2 pizzas
  Ⓒ 1 pizza
  Ⓓ 4 pizzas

8. There are 27 apples. How many pies can be made if each pie uses 3 apples?

  Ⓐ 7 pies
  Ⓑ 8 pies
  Ⓒ 9 pies
  Ⓓ 10 pies

9. Keegan is planting a garden in even rows. He has 48 seeds. Which layout is NOT possible?

  Ⓐ 6 rows of 8 seeds
  Ⓑ 8 rows of 6 seeds
  Ⓒ 7 rows of 7 seeds
  Ⓓ 12 rows of 4 seeds

10. There are 25 students in a gym class. They want to play a game with 5 equal teams. How many students will be on each team?

  Ⓐ 4 students
  Ⓑ 5 students
  Ⓒ 7 students
  Ⓓ 3 students

11. Josie has 7 days to read a book with 21 chapters. How many chapters should she read each day?

    Ⓐ 3 chapters
    Ⓑ 4 chapters
    Ⓒ 5 chapters
    Ⓓ 7 chapters

12. Devon has $40 to spend on fuel. One gallon of fuel costs $5. How many gallons can Devon afford to buy?

    Ⓐ 5 gallons
    Ⓑ 12 gallons
    Ⓒ 9 gallons
    Ⓓ 8 gallons

13. Amanda is using the following cake recipe:
    4 cups flour
    1 cup sugar
    3 cups milk
    1 egg
    If Amanda needs to make three batches, how many cups of flour will she need?

    Ⓐ 7 cups
    Ⓑ 12 cups
    Ⓒ 10 cups
    Ⓓ 16 cups

14. Kim invited 20 friends to her birthday party. Twice as many friends than she invited showed up the day of the party. Which number sentence could be used to solve how many friends came to the party?

    Ⓐ n + 20 = 2
    Ⓑ n x 20 = 2
    Ⓒ 20 x 2 = n
    Ⓓ 20 - n = 20

15. The product of 9 and a number is 45.
    Which number sentence models this situation?

    Ⓐ 9 + n = 45
    Ⓑ 45 + 9 = n
    Ⓒ 9 x n = 45
    Ⓓ 5 x n = 45

16. A classroom has 5 rows of desks. There are 6 desks in each row. How many desks are there altogether? Select the number sentences that represent the solution. Choose all correct answers.

    Ⓐ 6 - 5 = 1
    Ⓑ 5 x 6 = 30
    Ⓒ 6 x 5 = 30
    Ⓓ 5 + 6 = 11

17. Jasmine bought a bouquet of 24 flowers. She plans to give the same number of flowers to her 4 friends, Daniel, Raquel, Elliot and Sue. How many flowers will each friend receive? Circle the correct answer.

    Ⓐ 2
    Ⓑ 5
    Ⓒ 6
    Ⓓ 4

18. There are 48 cupcakes to be shared equally among 6 boys. How many cupcakes will each boy get? Write your answer in the box given below.

19. PART A
    Fill in the blank with the correct symbol to make this equation true.

    $64 \div 8 = 2 \_\_\_ 4.$

    PART B
    Fill in the blank with the correct symbol to make this equation true.

    $2 \_\_\_ 4 = 42 \div 7.$

20. Joseph reads 8 pages every day. In how many days will he be able to complete reading a book which has 56 pages? Write an equation to represent this in the box below, and find the number of days Joseph takes to complete the book.

Name _____   **Date** _____

Chapter 2

Lesson 4: Finding Unknown Values

You can scan the QR code given below or use the url to access additional EdSearch resources including videos and mobile apps related to *Finding Unknown Values*.

 Finding Unknown Values

URL	QR Code
http://www.lumoslearning.com/a/3oaa4	

1. **Find the number that makes this equation true.**
   n x 6 = 30

   Ⓐ n = 11
   Ⓑ n = 7
   Ⓒ n = 5
   Ⓓ n = 3

2. **Find the number that makes this equation true.**
   7 x ___ = 21

   Ⓐ 3
   Ⓑ 4
   Ⓒ 5
   Ⓓ 6

3. **Find the number that makes this equation true.**
   ___ x 4 = 36

   Ⓐ 9
   Ⓑ 8
   Ⓒ 7
   Ⓓ 6

4. **Find the number that makes this equation true.**
   n ÷ 9 = 8

   Ⓐ n = 81
   Ⓑ n = 45
   Ⓒ n = 72
   Ⓓ n = 63

5. **Find the number that makes this equation true.**
   ___ ÷ 3 = 10

   Ⓐ 27
   Ⓑ 30
   Ⓒ 33
   Ⓓ 60

6. Find the number that makes this equation true.
$45 \div n = 9$

Ⓐ n = 10
Ⓑ n = 7
Ⓒ n = 5
Ⓓ n = 3

7. Find the number that makes this equation true.
$64 = \underline{\quad} \times 8$

Ⓐ 6
Ⓑ 7
Ⓒ 8
Ⓓ 9

8. Find the number that makes this equation true.
$12 \div \underline{\quad} = 2$

Ⓐ 7
Ⓑ 6
Ⓒ 8
Ⓓ 4

9. Find the number that makes this equation true.
$\underline{\quad} \div 7 = 11$

Ⓐ 63
Ⓑ 70
Ⓒ 77
Ⓓ 78

10. Find the number that makes this equation true.
$16 = n \times 4$

Ⓐ n = 12
Ⓑ n = 4
Ⓒ n = 3
Ⓓ n = 2

11. For what value of m is this equation true?
    m x 7 = 56

    Ⓐ m = 6
    Ⓑ m = 8
    Ⓒ m = 7
    Ⓓ m = 12

12. For what value of n is this equation true?
    60 ÷ n = 5

    Ⓐ n = 8
    Ⓑ n = 12
    Ⓒ n = 14
    Ⓓ n = 16

13. For what value of z is this equation true?
    9 x z = 81

    Ⓐ z = 11
    Ⓑ z = 9
    Ⓒ z = 12
    Ⓓ z = 7

14. For what value of p is this equation true?
    p ÷ 3 = 3

    Ⓐ p = 6
    Ⓑ p = 1
    Ⓒ p = 9
    Ⓓ p = 0

15. For what value of u is this equation true?
    10 ÷ u = 10

    Ⓐ u = 1
    Ⓑ u = 0
    Ⓒ u = 10
    Ⓓ u = 100

16. ___ ÷ 6 = 9

Which number makes the equation true? Write your answer in the box given.

17. ___ x ___ = 14

Which numbers will make the equation true? Select all correct answers.

Ⓐ 5
Ⓑ 7
Ⓒ 6
Ⓓ 2

18. Enter the correct answer in the table.

Equation	Product
4 x 8=	
	x 7 = 63
3 x 5=	
	x 1 =7

19. PART A

A pen costs $7 to buy. How much would six pens cost? Write an equation to represent this in the box below.

PART B

Use the equation from **PART A** to find the cost of six pens.

20. Match the value of n for each of the equations given.

Equation	n=7	n=6
3 × 8 = 4 × n	○	○
72 ÷ 9 = 56 ÷ n	○	○

Chapter 2

Lesson 5: Multiplication & Division Properties

You can scan the QR code given below or use the url to access additional EdSearch resources including videos and mobile apps related to *Multiplication & Division Properties.*

 Multiplication & Division Properties

URL	QR Code
http://www.lumoslearning.com/a/3oab5	

1. Which of these statements is not true?

   Ⓐ 4 x (3 x 6) = (4 x 3) x 6
   Ⓑ 4 x 3 = 3 x 4
   Ⓒ 15 x 0 = 0 x 15
   Ⓓ 12 x 1 = 12 x 12

2. Which of these statements is true?

   Ⓐ The product of 11 x 6 is equal to the product of 6 x 11.
   Ⓑ The product of 11 x 6 is greater than the product of 6 x 11.
   Ⓒ The product of 11 x 6 is less than the product of 6 x 11.
   Ⓓ There is no relationship between the product of 11 x 6 and the product of 6 x 11.

3. Which of the following expressions has a value of 0?

   Ⓐ (3 x 4) x 1
   Ⓑ 50 x 1
   Ⓒ 3 x 4 x 0
   Ⓓ (3 x 1) x 2

4. Select the option in which both the numerical expressions result in a value of 0?

   Ⓐ 60 x 1 and 1 x 60
   Ⓑ 10 x 10 and 0 x 10
   Ⓒ 27 x 0 and 0 x 27
   Ⓓ 0 ÷ 15 and 15 ÷ 15

5. Which mathematical property does this equation model?
   6 x 1 = 6

   Ⓐ Commutative Property of Multiplication
   Ⓑ Associative Property of Multiplication
   Ⓒ Identity Property of Multiplication
   Ⓓ Distributive Property

6. Which mathematical property does this equation model?
   9 x 6 = 6 x 9

   Ⓐ Commutative Property of Multiplication
   Ⓑ Associative Property of Multiplication
   Ⓒ Identity Property of Multiplication
   Ⓓ Distributive Property

7. Which mathematical property does this equation model?
   (2 x 10) x 3 = 2 x (10 x 3)

   Ⓐ Commutative Property of Multiplication
   Ⓑ Associative Property of Multiplication
   Ⓒ Identity Property of Multiplication
   Ⓓ Distributive Property

8. Which mathematical property does this equation model?
   4 x (9 + 6) = (4 x 9) + (4 x 6)

   Ⓐ Commutative Property of Multiplication
   Ⓑ Associative Property of Multiplication
   Ⓒ Identity Property of Multiplication
   Ⓓ Distributive Property

9. By the Commutative Property of Multiplication, if you know that 4 x 5= 20, then you also know that _____ .

   Ⓐ 20 is an even number
   Ⓑ 4 x 6 = 24
   Ⓒ 5 x 4 = 20
   Ⓓ 5 is greater than 4

10. By the Associative Property of Multiplication, If you know that (2 x 3) x 4 = 24, then you also know that _____.

    Ⓐ 2 x (3 x 4) = 24
    Ⓑ 2 x 4 = 8
    Ⓒ 24 ÷ 6 = 4
    Ⓓ (2 x 3) x 5 = 30

11. Complete the following statement:
    Multiplication and _____ are inverse operations.

    Ⓐ addition
    Ⓑ subtraction
    Ⓒ division
    Ⓓ distribution

12. 32 x 7 = 7 x 32
    This equation models the _____.

    Ⓐ Commutative Property of Multiplication
    Ⓑ Associative Property of Multiplication
    Ⓒ Identity Property of Multiplication
    Ⓓ Distributive Property

13. 26 x 2 = (20 x 2) + (6 x 2)
    This equation models the _____ .

    Ⓐ Commutative Property of Multiplication
    Ⓑ Associative Property of Multiplication
    Ⓒ Identity Property of Multiplication
    Ⓓ Distributive Property

14. By the Identity Property of Multiplication, you know that _____.

    Ⓐ 2 x 2 = 4
    Ⓑ 0 x 0 = 0
    Ⓒ 6 x 1 = 6
    Ⓓ 5 ÷ 5 = 1

15. What number belongs in the blank?
    10 x __ = 10

    Ⓐ 1
    Ⓑ 0
    Ⓒ 10
    Ⓓ 5

16. From the below 4 options, select 2 options that will result in the same product based on
    the commutative property of multiplication?

    Ⓐ 5 + 4
    Ⓑ 10 x 2
    Ⓒ 5 x 4
    Ⓓ 4 x 5

17. Make the equation true according to the Identity Property of Multiplication. Write the correct number in the answer box given below.

7 x ___ = 7

18. (2 x 3) x 4 = 24 and 2 x (3 x 4) = 24

Identify the property that is applicable. Circle the correct answer choice.

Ⓐ Associative property of multiplication
Ⓑ Distributive property
Ⓒ Commutative property of multiplication
Ⓓ Identity Property of Multiplication

19. PART A:

Which number will make the below equation true. Write your answer in the box given below.

3 x 7 = 7 x ?

PART B:

Which property did you use in Part A to arrive at the answer. Write the name of the property in the box given below.

20. Match the property with the correct example.

	3 x (5 x 7) = (3 x 5) x 7	3 x 1 = 3	3 x 5 = 5 x 3	3 x (5 + 7) = (3 x 5) + (3 x 7)
Commutative Property	○	○	○	○
Associative Property	○	○	○	○
Identity Property	○	○	○	○
Distributive Property	○	○	○	○

Chapter 2

Lesson 6: Relating Multiplication & Division

You can scan the QR code given below or use the url to access additional EdSearch resources including videos and mobile apps related to Relating *Multiplication & Division*.

 **Relating Multiplication & Division**

URL	QR Code
http://www.lumoslearning.com/a/3oab6	

1. Find the number that would complete both of the following number sentences.
   ___ x 6 = 30
   30 ÷ 6 = ___

   Ⓐ 7
   Ⓑ 5
   Ⓒ 6
   Ⓓ 24

2. Find the number that would complete both of the following number sentences.
   7 x ___ = 21
   21 ÷ ___ = 7

   Ⓐ 5
   Ⓑ 14
   Ⓒ 3
   Ⓓ 7

3. Find the number that would complete both of the following number sentences.
   72 ÷ ___ = 8
   8 x ___ = 72

   Ⓐ 8
   Ⓑ 9
   Ⓒ 10
   Ⓓ 64

4. Find the number that would complete both of the following number sentences.
   50 ÷ ___ = 5
   ___ x 5 = 50

   Ⓐ 15
   Ⓑ 5
   Ⓒ 45
   Ⓓ 10

5. Find the number that would complete both of the following number sentences.
   36 ÷ ___ =
   ___ x 9 = 36

   Ⓐ 4
   Ⓑ 5
   Ⓒ 27
   Ⓓ 9

6. There are 9 students in a group. Each student needs 5 sheets of paper to complete a project. Which number sentence below can be used to find out how many total sheets of paper are needed for this project? Select all the correct answer choices.

   Ⓐ 5 x _____ = 9
   Ⓑ 9 x 5 = _____
   Ⓒ _____ ÷ 5 = 9
   Ⓓ 9 ÷ 5 = _____

7. In a football game, Timmy scored 8 touchdowns. Each touchdown was worth 7 points. Which number sentence below can be used to find out how many points Timmy scored in all?

   Ⓐ 56 x _____ = 8
   Ⓑ _____ ÷ 7 = 8
   Ⓒ 7 x 56 = _____
   Ⓓ 8 ÷ 7 = _____

8. Devon needs to buy 96 pencils for his goodie bags. Pencils are sold in packages of 12. Which number sentence below can be used to find out how many packages Devon needs to buy?

   Ⓐ 12 ÷ 96 = _____
   Ⓑ 12 x 96 = _____
   Ⓒ _____ x 12 = 96
   Ⓓ 12 ÷ _____ = 96

9. Eighty-four students are attending an awards ceremony. They are to be seated at twelve equal tables. Which number sentence below can be used to find out how many students should be assigned to each table?

   Ⓐ 6 x _____ = 84
   Ⓑ 12 x _____ = 84
   Ⓒ 84 x 12 = _____
   Ⓓ 12 ÷ 84 = _____

10. Walter has 16 slices of pizza to share among himself and seven friends. He wants each person to get an equal number of slices. Which number sentence below can be used to find out how many slices each person will get?

   Ⓐ 7 ÷ 16 = _____
   Ⓑ 7 x 16 = _____
   Ⓒ 7 x _____ = 16
   Ⓓ 8 x _____ = 16

11. Which of the following equations would be in the same fact family as:
    6 x 5 = 30?

    Ⓐ 30 ÷ 10 = 3
    Ⓑ 6 x 30 = 5
    Ⓒ 30 ÷ 5 = 6
    Ⓓ 5 ÷ 30 = 6

12. Which number sentence is equivalent to the number sentence below?
    4 x n = 32

    Ⓐ 4 x 32 = n
    Ⓑ n + 4 = 32
    Ⓒ 32 ÷ 4 = n
    Ⓓ 4 x 4 = n

13. Which number sentence is equivalent to the number sentence below?
    n x 6 = 48

    Ⓐ 48 x n = 6
    Ⓑ 6 x 4 = n
    Ⓒ 48 x 6 = n
    Ⓓ 48 ÷ n = 6

14. Which number sentence is equivalent to the number sentence below?
    45 ÷ n = 9

    Ⓐ 9 x 45 = n
    Ⓑ 45 x n = 9
    Ⓒ 9 x n = 45
    Ⓓ n + 9 = 45

15. David receives 2 pieces of candy for each chore that he completes each week. This week he earned 32 pieces of candy. Which number sentence below can be used to figure out how many chores David completed?

    Ⓐ 2 x 32 = ___
    Ⓑ ___ x 2 = 32
    Ⓒ 32 + 2 = ___
    Ⓓ 2 ÷ 32 = ___

16. Match each multiplication sentence with the corresponding division sentence.
    Remember, if a x b= c then c ÷ a= b.

	40÷5=8	36÷6=6	21÷7=3	18÷9=2
6 x 6= 36	○	○	○	○
9 x 2= 18	○	○	○	○
5 x 8= 40	○	○	○	○
7 x 3= 21	○	○	○	○

17. Complete the table by typing in the correct number. Remember, if a x b= c then c ÷ a= b.

	Division Expression	Quotient
If 4 x 4= 16 then...	16 ÷ 4=	
If 7 x 6= 42 then... 42 ÷		6
If 3 x 9= 27 then...		÷ 3=9

18. Which multiplication sentences relate to 63 ÷ 9= 7? Select all the correct answers.
    Note: More than one option may be correct.

    Ⓐ 7 x 7= 49
    Ⓑ 7 x 9= 63
    Ⓒ 9 x 7= 63
    Ⓓ 9 x 8= 72

19. Which number sentence is equivalent to the number sentence below:

    65 ÷ n = 5.

    Ⓐ 65=5 × n
    Ⓑ 65=5 ÷ n
    Ⓒ 65=n ÷ 5
    Ⓓ 65=5 - n

20. Part A

For the expression below, Circle the correct symbol to be filled in the blank.

40 ÷ 5 ____ 54 ÷ 9

Ⓐ =
Ⓑ >
Ⓒ <

Part B

For the expression below, Circle the correct symbol to be filled in the blank.

35 ÷ 7 ____ 28 ÷ 4

Ⓐ =
Ⓑ >
Ⓒ <

Part C

For the expression below, Circle the correct symbol to be filled in the blank.

18 ÷ 6 ____ 24 ÷ 8

Ⓐ =
Ⓑ >
Ⓒ <

Chapter 2

Lesson 7: Multiplication & Division Facts

You can scan the QR code given below or use the url to access additional EdSearch resources including videos and mobile apps related to *Multiplication & Division Facts*.

 Multiplication & Division Facts

URL	QR Code
http://www.lumoslearning.com/a/3oac7	

1. **Find the product.**
   6 x 0 = ____

   (A) 6
   (B) 1
   (C) 0
   (D) 2

2. **Find the product.**
   1 x 10 = ____

   (A) 0
   (B) 1
   (C) 10
   (D) 11

3. **Solve.**
   3 x 8 = ____

   (A) 24
   (B) 21
   (C) 18
   (D) 28

4. **Solve.**
   ____ = 5 x 9

   (A) 40
   (B) 45
   (C) 50
   (D) 35

5. **Find the product of 8 and 6.**

   (A) 14
   (B) 42
   (C) 48
   (D) 56

6. **Find the product of 7 and 7.**

   Ⓐ 42
   Ⓑ 46
   Ⓒ 49
   Ⓓ 56

7. **Find the product of 4 and 6.**

   Ⓐ 20
   Ⓑ 24
   Ⓒ 28
   Ⓓ 32

8. **Find the product.**
   6 x 9 = ____

   Ⓐ 54
   Ⓑ 45
   Ⓒ 48
   Ⓓ 64

9. **Find the product.**
   ____ = 9 x 8

   Ⓐ 64
   Ⓑ 72
   Ⓒ 81
   Ⓓ 82

10. **Which expression below has a product of 48?**

   Ⓐ 6 x 7
   Ⓑ 4 x 14
   Ⓒ 7 x 8
   Ⓓ 8 x 6

11. **Find the quotient of 25 and 5.**

   Ⓐ 20
   Ⓑ 5
   Ⓒ 4
   Ⓓ 15

12. What is 32 divided by 4?

Ⓐ 9

Ⓑ 8

Ⓒ 7

Ⓓ 6

13. What is 28 divided by 7?

Ⓐ 4

Ⓑ 5

Ⓒ 3

Ⓓ 6

14. Find the quotient.
0 ÷ 5 = ____

Ⓐ 0

Ⓑ 1

Ⓒ 5

Ⓓ 50

15. Find the quotient.
7 ÷ 1 = ____

Ⓐ 1

Ⓑ 0

Ⓒ 7

Ⓓ 8

16. Find the quotient.
____ = 12 ÷ 2

Ⓐ 9

Ⓑ 8

Ⓒ 7

Ⓓ 6

17. Divide.
63 ÷ 9 = ____

Ⓐ 6

Ⓑ 7

Ⓒ 8

Ⓓ 9

18. Divide.
42 ÷ 7 = _____

Ⓐ 5
Ⓑ 6
Ⓒ 7
Ⓓ 8

19. Find the quotient of 33 and 3.

Ⓐ 11
Ⓑ 12
Ⓒ 10
Ⓓ 9

20. Divide.
56 ÷ 7 = _____

Ⓐ 6
Ⓑ 7
Ⓒ 8
Ⓓ 9

21. Solve.
4 x 12 = _____

Ⓐ 36
Ⓑ 48
Ⓒ 42
Ⓓ 46

22. Solve.
_____ = 75 ÷ 5

Ⓐ 13
Ⓑ 15
Ⓒ 17
Ⓓ 25

23. Solve.
84 ÷ 12 = _____

Ⓐ 7
Ⓑ 8
Ⓒ 9
Ⓓ 12

24. Solve.

12 x 3 = ____

Ⓐ 32
Ⓑ 36
Ⓒ 39
Ⓓ 48

25. Solve.

36 ÷ 3 = ____

Ⓐ 22
Ⓑ 12
Ⓒ 14
Ⓓ 18

26. Solve.

60 ÷ 5 = ____

Ⓐ 8
Ⓑ 9
Ⓒ 12
Ⓓ 14

27. Solve.

11 x 4 = ____

Ⓐ 32
Ⓑ 44
Ⓒ 39
Ⓓ 46

28. Solve.

____ = 80 ÷ 8

Ⓐ 10
Ⓑ 9
Ⓒ 8
Ⓓ 12

29. Solve.

12 x 8 = _____

Ⓐ 72
Ⓑ 84
Ⓒ 92
Ⓓ 96

30. Solve.

50 ÷ 5 = _____

Ⓐ 25
Ⓑ 20
Ⓒ 10
Ⓓ 50

31. Match each equation to the correct product.

	12	18	32
6 x 3=	○	○	○
8 x 4=	○	○	○
4 x 3=	○	○	○
9 x 2=	○	○	○

32. 24 ÷ 4=?

Write the answer in the box given below.

33. Which expressions have a product of 36. Select all the correct answers.

Ⓐ 6 x 6
Ⓑ 8 x 4
Ⓒ 6 x 8
Ⓓ 9 x 4

34. Find the quotient. 27 ÷ 9 = ? Circle the correct answer.

Ⓐ 18
Ⓑ 4
Ⓒ 3
Ⓓ 2

35. Complete the following table.

5	x	8	=	
8	÷		=	8
	÷	7	=	0
6	x		=	30

Chapter 2

Lesson 8: Two-Step Problems

You can scan the QR code given below or use the url to access additional EdSearch resources including videos and mobile apps related to *Two-Step Problems*.

 Two-Step Problems

URL	QR Code
http://www.lumoslearning.com/a/3oad8	

1. Danny has 47 baseball cards. He gives his brother 11 cards. Danny then divides the remaining cards between 3 of his classmates. How many cards does each classmate receive?

   Ⓐ 15
   Ⓑ 3
   Ⓒ 12
   Ⓓ 11

2. Two classes of grade three students are lined up outside. One class is lined up in 3 rows of 7. The other class is lined up in 4 rows of 5. How many total third graders are lined up outside?

   Ⓐ 19 third graders
   Ⓑ 21 third graders
   Ⓒ 41 third graders
   Ⓓ 20 third graders

3. Jessica earns 10 dollars per hour for babysitting. She has saved 60 dollars so far. How many more hours will she need to babysit to buy something that costs 100 dollars?

   Ⓐ 40 hours
   Ⓑ 6 hours
   Ⓒ 10 hours
   Ⓓ 4 hours

4. George started with 2 bags of 10 cookies. He gave 12 cookies to his parents. How many cookies does George have now?

   Ⓐ 8 cookies
   Ⓑ 10 cookies
   Ⓒ 12 cookies
   Ⓓ 20 cookies

5. Renae has 60 minutes to do her chores and do her homework. She has 3 chores to complete and each chore takes 15 minutes to complete. After completing her chores, how many minutes does Renae have left to do her homework?

   Ⓐ 15 minutes
   Ⓑ 45 minutes
   Ⓒ 30 minutes
   Ⓓ 0 minutes

6. Anna and Jamie want to buy a new board game. The original cost was 28 dollars. It is on sale for 4 dollars off. How much money should each girl pay if they buy the game on sale and pay equal amounts?

    Ⓐ $24
    Ⓑ $2
    Ⓒ $12
    Ⓓ $14

7. 100 students went on a field trip. Ten students rode with their parents in a car while the remaining students were divided equally into 5 buses. How many students rode on each bus?

    Ⓐ 9 students
    Ⓑ 18 students
    Ⓒ 50 students
    Ⓓ 90 students

8. Julia has 32 books. Her sister has twice the number of books that Julia has. How many books do the girls have altogether?

    Ⓐ 66 books
    Ⓑ 32 books
    Ⓒ 64 books
    Ⓓ 96 books

9. Alicia bought 5 crates of apples. Each crate had 8 apples. She divided the apples equally into 10 bags. How many apples were in each bag?

    Ⓐ 40 apples
    Ⓑ 4 apples
    Ⓒ 10 apples
    Ⓓ 5 apples

10. Janeth went to the store and spent 4 dollars on markers. She also bought 3 copies of the same book. If she spent a total of 19 dollars, how much did each book cost?

    Ⓐ 5 dollars
    Ⓑ 4 dollars
    Ⓒ 3 dollars
    Ⓓ 6 dollars

11. Brian won 24 candy bars in a contest. He gave 2 candy bars to each of his 7 friends. How many candy bars does Brian have left?

   Ⓐ 14 candy bars
   Ⓑ 12 candy bars
   Ⓒ 10 candy bars
   Ⓓ 17 candy bars

12. Jenine gave 3 mini cupcakes to each of her three sisters. She then had 4 left for herself. How many mini cupcakes did Jenine start with?

   Ⓐ 13 mini cupcakes
   Ⓑ 9 mini cupcakes
   Ⓒ 10 mini cupcakes
   Ⓓ 7 mini cupcakes

13. Twenty-two people visited the art exhibit at the museum on Friday. Twice as many people visited on Saturday. How many people combined visited the art exhibit at the museum on Friday and Saturday?

   Ⓐ 88 people
   Ⓑ 66 people
   Ⓒ 22 people
   Ⓓ 44 people

14. Audrey can watch 5 hours of TV a week. She has already watched 4 shows that are each 1 hour long. How many more hours can she watch TV this week?

   Ⓐ 3 hours
   Ⓑ 2 hours
   Ⓒ 1 hour
   Ⓓ 4 hours

15. Greg had 3 books. His older brother gave him 15 more books. Greg wants to divide his total number of books equally onto 6 shelves. How many books should he place on each shelf?

   Ⓐ 3 books
   Ⓑ 12 books
   Ⓒ 18 books
   Ⓓ 6 books

16. Sarah bought 2 boxes of doughnuts. Each box contained 12 donuts. She shared a total of 7 donuts with her friends. How many doughnuts does she have now? Identify which equations can be used to find the answer. (Choose all correct answers)

Ⓐ 12 x 2= 24
Ⓑ 12 + 2= 14
Ⓒ 24-7= 17
Ⓓ 2 + 12 + 7= 21

17. Freddy has a collection of 32 baseball cards. He wants to share the cards with 4 classmates. One of the classmates brings 8 more cards to add to the collection. If Freddy and his classmates share all the cards, each receiving the same number, how many cards does each person have? What should be the steps to be followed to arrive at the answer? Write the steps in the correct sequence in the boxes given below.

Ⓐ 32 - 6 = 26
Ⓑ 4 + 1 = 5
Ⓒ 32 + 8 = 40
Ⓓ 40 ÷ 5 = 8

18. A farmer collected 22 pints of milk from his cows. He put all the milk into bottles. Each bottle holds 2 pints of milk. He accidentally spilled 6 bottles of milk. How many bottles are left with the farmer now? Circle the math sentences that can be used to find the answer. (Circle all correct answers)

Ⓐ 11
Ⓑ 24
Ⓒ 16
Ⓓ 5

19. For each of the problems in the first column, select the correct answer.

	$50	$5	$10	$4
Karen had 86 dollars. He bought 7 books. After buying them he had 16 dollars. How much did each book cost ?	○	○	○	○
Jose and his four friends bought a new board game. It was on sale for 20 dollars off. If each of the boys (total 5 of them) paid $6. What was the original cost of the new board game?	○	○	○	○
A shopkeeper buys 5 pens for $35 and sells them at the rate of $8 per pen. If he sells all the five pens, how much profit he will get?	○	○	○	○
Jeffrey bought 8 actions figures which cost 3 dollars each from John. John bought 6 books from the amount he received from Jeffrey. If the cost of each book John purchased is the same, what is the cost of each book?	○	○	○	○

Chapter 2

Lesson 9: Number Patterns

You can scan the QR code given below or use the url to access additional EdSearch resources including videos and mobile apps related to *Number Patterns*.

 **Number Patterns**

URL	QR Code
http://www.lumoslearning.com/a/3oad9	

1. Which of the following is an even number?

   Ⓐ 764,723
   Ⓑ 90,835
   Ⓒ 5,862
   Ⓓ 609

2. Which of these sets contains no odd numbers?

   Ⓐ 13, 15, 81, 109, 199
   Ⓑ 123, 133, 421, 412, 600
   Ⓒ 34, 46, 48, 106, 88
   Ⓓ 12, 37, 6, 14, 144

3. Complete the following statement.
   The sum of two even numbers will always be _____ .

   Ⓐ greater than 10
   Ⓑ less than 100
   Ⓒ even
   Ⓓ odd

4. Complete the following statement.
   The product of two even numbers will always be _____ .

   Ⓐ even
   Ⓑ odd
   Ⓒ a multiple of 10
   Ⓓ a square number

5. Complete the following statement.
   A number has a nine in its ones place. The number must be a multiple of _____.

   Ⓐ 9
   Ⓑ 3
   Ⓒ 7
   Ⓓ None of the above

6. Complete the following statement.
   Numbers that are multiples of 8 are all _____.

   Ⓐ even
   Ⓑ multiples of 2
   Ⓒ multiples of 4
   Ⓓ All of the above

7. If this pattern continues, what will the next 3 numbers be?
   7, 14, 21, 28, 35, ...

   Ⓐ 41, 47, 53
   Ⓑ 49, 56, 63
   Ⓒ 77, 84, 91
   Ⓓ 42, 49, 56

8. Complete the following statement.
   All multiples of _____ can be decomposed into two equal addends.

   Ⓐ 6
   Ⓑ 9
   Ⓒ 3
   Ⓓ 5

9. If this pattern continues, what will the next 3 numbers be?
   9, 18, 27, 36, ...

   Ⓐ 54, 63, 72
   Ⓑ 45, 54, 63
   Ⓒ 44, 52, 60
   Ⓓ 44, 53, 62

10. A number is multiplied by 7 and the resulting product is even. Which of these could have been the number?

   Ⓐ 7
   Ⓑ 17
   Ⓒ 34
   Ⓓ 99

11. Complete the following statement.
    The multiples of 4 will always _____.

    Ⓐ have a 2 in the ones place
    Ⓑ be even
    Ⓒ be divisible by 8
    Ⓓ None of these

12. Complete the following statement.
    The sum of an even number and an odd number will always be _____.

    Ⓐ even
    Ⓑ odd
    Ⓒ divisible by 3
    Ⓓ None of the above

13. Complete the following statement.
    A multiple of 4 can have a _____ in its ones place.

    Ⓐ 2
    Ⓑ 8
    Ⓒ 6
    Ⓓ All of the above

14. Complete the following statement.
    A multiple of 5 can have a _____ as its ones digit.

    Ⓐ 0
    Ⓑ 3
    Ⓒ 9
    Ⓓ All of the above

15. Which of the following would produce an even product?

    Ⓐ an even number times an even number
    Ⓑ an even number times an odd number
    Ⓒ an odd number times an even number
    Ⓓ All of the above

16. Select the number that will come next if the pattern continues.

	10	35	24
2, 4, 6, 8	○	○	○
40, 36, 32, 28	○	○	○
7, 14, 21, 28	○	○	○

17. Type in the numbers that complete the table if the pattern is multiples of 3.

IN	OUT
3	9
4	
5	15
	18
7	

18. If the pattern continues, which of the following numbers will appear?
    Note: More than one option may be correct.

    100, 90, 80, 70

    Ⓐ 50
    Ⓑ 110
    Ⓒ 80
    Ⓓ 60

19. Complete the following statement. If you subtract an odd number from an even number, the difference will always be (a/an) _____. Circle the correct answer.

    Ⓐ Multiple of 3
    Ⓑ Even number
    Ⓒ Odd number
    Ⓓ Odd number or Even number

20. For each statement in the first column, choose all the correct answers.

	2	4	5	7
A number has a four in its ones place. The number can be a multiple of _____.	○	○	○	○
A number has a five in its ones place. The number can be a multiple of _____.	○	○	○	○
A number has a zero in its ones place. The number can be a multiple of _____.	○	○	○	○
A number has a three in its ones place. The number can be a multiple of _____.	○	○	○	○

End of Operations and Algebraic Thinking

Chapter 3:
Number & Operations in Base Ten

Lesson 1: Rounding Numbers

You can scan the QR code given below or use the url to access additional EdSearch resources including videos and mobile apps related to *Rounding Numbers*.

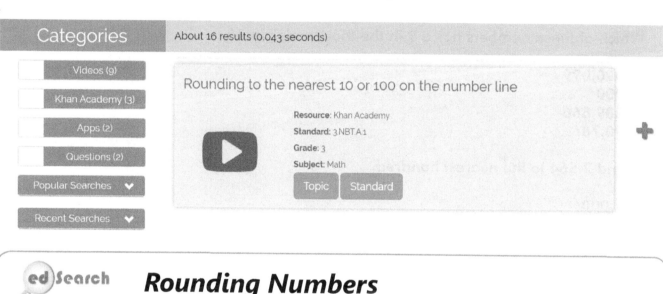

Categories   About 16 results (0.043 seconds)

Videos (9)

Khan Academy (3)

Apps (2)

Questions (2)

Popular Searches ⌄

Recent Searches ⌄

Rounding to the nearest 10 or 100 on the number line

Resource: Khan Academy
Standard: 3.NBT.A.1
Grade: 3
Subject: Math

Topic   Standard

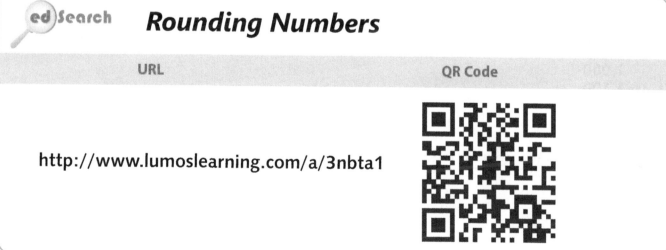

ed)Search   *Rounding Numbers*

URL	QR Code
http://www.lumoslearning.com/a/3nbta1	

1. What is the value of the 9 in 11,291?

   Ⓐ 9 ones
   Ⓑ 9 hundreds
   Ⓒ 9 thousands
   Ⓓ 9 tens

2. What is the value of the digit 6 in 36,801?

   Ⓐ Six thousand
   Ⓑ Sixty
   Ⓒ Sixty thousand
   Ⓓ Six hundred

3. Which of these numbers has a 9 in the thousands place?

   Ⓐ 690,099
   Ⓑ 900
   Ⓒ 209,866
   Ⓓ 90,786

4. Round 2,564 to the nearest hundred.

   Ⓐ 2,000
   Ⓑ 2,500
   Ⓒ 2,600
   Ⓓ 2,700

5. Round 1,043 to the nearest hundred.

   Ⓐ 1,000
   Ⓑ 1,100
   Ⓒ 1,040
   Ⓓ 1,200

6. Round 537 to the nearest ten.

   Ⓐ 500
   Ⓑ 540
   Ⓒ 550
   Ⓓ 530

7. **Round 957 to the nearest ten.**

    Ⓐ 960
    Ⓑ 950
    Ⓒ 900
    Ⓓ 1,000

8. **Maya is buying pencils for the school. Maya needs to buy enough pencils for 388 students. What is this number rounded to the nearest hundred?**

    Ⓐ 390
    Ⓑ 380
    Ⓒ 400
    Ⓓ 500

9. **Ninety-seven chairs are needed for an audience. What is this number rounded to the nearest ten?**

    Ⓐ 90
    Ⓑ 100
    Ⓒ 80
    Ⓓ 110

10. **Which of the following numbers does not round to 1,000 when rounding to the nearest hundred?**

    Ⓐ 955
    Ⓑ 1,005
    Ⓒ 1,051
    Ⓓ 951

11. **How many whole numbers, when rounded to the nearest ten give 100 as the result?**

    Ⓐ 8
    Ⓑ 9
    Ⓒ 10
    Ⓓ 11

12. **Fill in the blank.**
    795 rounds to 800 when rounded to the nearest _____.

    Ⓐ ten
    Ⓑ hundred
    Ⓒ ten or hundred
    Ⓓ thousand

13. Fill in the blank.
1,090 rounds to 1,100 when rounded to the nearest _____.

Ⓐ ten
Ⓑ hundred
Ⓒ ten or hundred
Ⓓ thousand

14. The attendance at a local baseball game is announced to be 4,328. What is this number rounded to the nearest ten?

Ⓐ 4,300
Ⓑ 4,330
Ⓒ 4,320
Ⓓ 4,400

15. The number of plants in a garden, when rounded to the nearest hundred, rounds to 800. Which of the following could not be the number of plants in the garden?

Ⓐ 850
Ⓑ 800
Ⓒ 750
Ⓓ 849

16. Which numbers represent the number 617 when rounded to the nearest ten or hundred? Circle all correct answers.

Ⓐ 620
Ⓑ 600
Ⓒ 700
Ⓓ 630

17. Round 489 to the nearest hundred. Write the correct answer into the box.

18. Complete the table in the format given in the example.

Number	Number when rounded to the nearest ten	Number when rounded to the nearest hundred
2,349	2,350	2,300
4,092		
8,396		

Chapter 3

Lesson 2: Addition & Subtraction

You can scan the QR code given below or use the url to access additional EdSearch resources including videos and mobile apps related to *Addition & Subtraction*.

 **Addition & Subtraction**

URL	QR Code
http://www.lumoslearning.com/a/3nbta2	

1. What is the standard form of 70,000 + 6,000 + 800 + 60 + 2?

   Ⓐ 706,862
   Ⓑ 76,862
   Ⓒ 7,682
   Ⓓ 782

2. Two numbers have a difference of 29. The two numbers could be _____.

   Ⓐ 11 and 18
   Ⓑ 23 and 42
   Ⓒ 40 and 11
   Ⓓ 50 and 39

3. Two numbers add up to 756. One number is 356. What is the other number?

   Ⓐ 356
   Ⓑ 300
   Ⓒ 400
   Ⓓ 456

4. Which of these expressions has the same difference as 94 - 50?

   Ⓐ 70 - 34
   Ⓑ 80 - 46
   Ⓒ 60 - 16
   Ⓓ 90 - 54

5. Which of these number sentences is not true?

   Ⓐ 88 + 12 = 90 + 10
   Ⓑ 82 + 18 = 88 + 12
   Ⓒ 56 + 45 = 54 + 56
   Ⓓ 46 + 15 = 56 + 5

6. Jim has 640 baseball cards and 280 basketball cards. How many sports cards does Jim have in all?

   Ⓐ 820 cards
   Ⓑ 360 cards
   Ⓒ 8,120 cards
   Ⓓ 920 cards

7. Find the difference.
   860 - 659

   Ⓐ 219
   Ⓑ 319
   Ⓒ 201
   Ⓓ 19

8. The students made 565 book covers for their math books. They used up 422 of the book covers. How many book covers are left?

   Ⓐ 242 book covers
   Ⓑ 163 book covers
   Ⓒ 987 book covers
   Ⓓ 143 book covers

9. What is the difference of 32 and 5?

   Ⓐ 33
   Ⓑ 27
   Ⓒ 160
   Ⓓ 37

10. Jenny plans to sell 50 boxes of cookies to help her scout troop raise funds. She sold 20 boxes to her neighbors. Her dad sold 15 boxes at his work office. How many more boxes does she need to sell to meet her goal?

    Ⓐ 15 boxes
    Ⓑ 10 boxes
    Ⓒ 5 boxes
    Ⓓ 25 boxes

11. Sara had 124 stickers. She gave away 62 stickers and bought 73 more stickers. How many stickers does Sara have now?

    Ⓐ 135 stickers
    Ⓑ 62 stickers
    Ⓒ 120 stickers
    Ⓓ 11 stickers

12. Which of these addition expressions would require regrouping of hundreds and tens?

    Ⓐ 923 + 37
    Ⓑ 456 + 443
    Ⓒ 235 + 234
    Ⓓ 576 + 442

13. There were 605 people sitting in an auditorium at the start of a show. Thirty-five people left during the intermission. How many people remained in the auditorium after the intermission?

Ⓐ 630 people
Ⓑ 580 people
Ⓒ 570 people
Ⓓ 595 people

14. If 3 tens are subtracted from 401, what is the difference?

Ⓐ 471
Ⓑ 371
Ⓒ 398
Ⓓ 381

15. Find the sum of 37 + 93 + 200.

Ⓐ 330
Ⓑ 663
Ⓒ 320
Ⓓ 300

16. Select the correct sum for each addition expression.

	899	467	558
422 + 136	○	○	○
608 + 291	○	○	○
157 + 310	○	○	○

17. Which of the following words refer to subtraction? Select all correct answers.

Ⓐ sum
Ⓑ difference
Ⓒ altogether
Ⓓ minus

18. Hannah received a score of 604 on the exam. Ben received a score of 719. What was the difference between the two scores? Write your answer in the box given below.

```
(                                                    )
```

19. Type in the correct numbers to make the sum true.

	Hundreds	Tens	Ones
	2		5
+		3	
Total	8	4	9

20. Karen has 805 milliliters of milk. After he drinks some milk, 538 milliliters are left. How much milk did Karen drink? Show the steps by which you arrive at the answer.

Chapter 3

Lesson 3: Multiplying Multiples of 10

You can scan the QR code given below or use the url to access additional EdSearch resources including videos and mobile apps related to *Multiplying Multiples of 10.*

 **Multiplying Multiples of 10**

URL	QR Code
http://www.lumoslearning.com/a/3nbta3	

1. **Multiply:**
   6 x 10 = ____

   Ⓐ 66
   Ⓑ 60
   Ⓒ 61
   Ⓓ 16

2. **What is the product of 10 and 10?**

   Ⓐ 20
   Ⓑ 50
   Ⓒ 100
   Ⓓ 1,000

3. **Find the product.**
   5 x 40 = _____

   Ⓐ 100
   Ⓑ 90
   Ⓒ 200
   Ⓓ 240

4. **Multiply:**
   ____ = 6 x 60

   Ⓐ 120
   Ⓑ 180
   Ⓒ 320
   Ⓓ 360

5. **Find the product of 70 and 7.**

   Ⓐ 77
   Ⓑ 140
   Ⓒ 420
   Ⓓ 490

6. **Multiply:**
   _____ = 30 x 7

   (A) 210
   (B) 240
   (C) 180
   (D) 100

7. **Find the product.**
   90 x 9 = _____

   (A) 800
   (B) 810
   (C) 900
   (D) 1,800

8. **Multiply:**
   8 x 80 = _____

   (A) 160
   (B) 620
   (C) 640
   (D) 660

9. **Find the product.**
   2 x 70 = _____

   (A) 140
   (B) 120
   (C) 90
   (D) 160

10. **Multiply:**
    90 x 3 = _____

    (A) 120
    (B) 180
    (C) 270
    (D) 290

11. Multiply:
   2 x 10 = ____

   Ⓐ 2
   Ⓑ 5
   Ⓒ 10
   Ⓓ 20

12. Multiply:
   50 x 1 = ____

   Ⓐ 1
   Ⓑ 25
   Ⓒ 49
   Ⓓ 50

13. Multiply:
   10 x 3 = ____

   Ⓐ 10
   Ⓑ 30
   Ⓒ 100
   Ⓓ 300

14. Find the product of 30 and 9.

   Ⓐ 270
   Ⓑ 39
   Ⓒ 3
   Ⓓ 100

15. Multiply:
   10 x 7 = ____

   Ⓐ 70
   Ⓑ 10
   Ⓒ 100
   Ⓓ 7

16. Select the math sentences that can be used to find the product of 70 and 5. Select all the relevant math sentences.

   Ⓐ 7 x 5 = 35
   Ⓑ 35 x 10= 350
   Ⓒ 70 x 50= 3,500
   Ⓓ 70 x 5= 350

17. Circle the picture that shows the product of 20 and 2.

   Instruction:

    = 10

Ⓐ

Ⓑ

Ⓒ

18. Find the product of 30 x 8. Write your answer in the box below.

19. Complete the following table:

a x b =	c
6 x 50 =	
8 x 60 =	
70 x 8 =	
80 x 9 =	

20. Match the multiplication expression with the correct product.

	630	320	540	450
9 x 60 =				
4 x 80 =				
90 x 5 =				
90 x 7 =				

End of Number & Operations in Base Ten

Chapter 4:
Number & Operations - Fractions

Lesson 1: Fractions of a Whole

You can scan the QR code given below or use the url to access additional EdSearch resources including videos and mobile apps related to *Fractions of a Whole*.

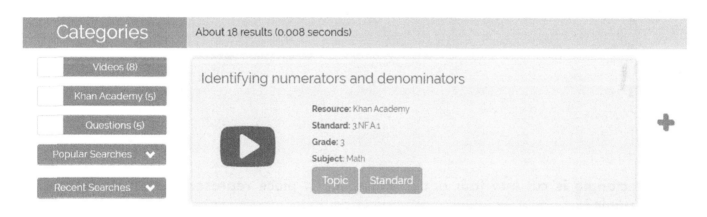

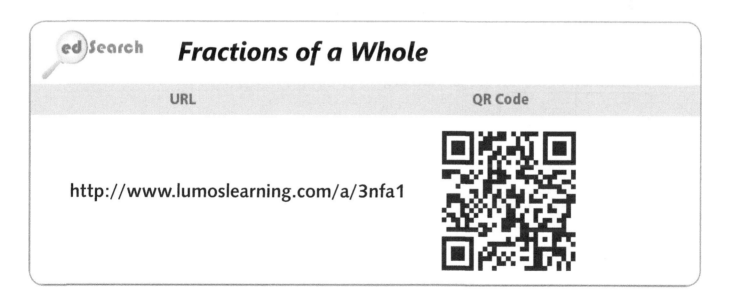

Fractions of a Whole

URL	QR Code
http://www.lumoslearning.com/a/3nfa1	

1. What fraction of the letters in the word "READING" are vowels?

    Ⓐ $\frac{4}{7}$

    Ⓑ $\frac{3}{4}$

    Ⓒ $\frac{3}{7}$

    Ⓓ $\frac{1}{3}$

2. A bag contains 3 red, 2 yellow, and 5 blue tiles. What fraction of the tiles are yellow?

    Ⓐ $\frac{2}{5}$

    Ⓑ $\frac{2}{10}$

    Ⓒ $\frac{3}{7}$

    Ⓓ $\frac{1}{3}$

3. A rectangle is cut into four equal pieces. Each piece represents what fraction of the rectangle?

    Ⓐ one half
    Ⓑ one third
    Ⓒ one fourth
    Ⓓ one fifth

4. What fraction of the square is shaded?

    Ⓐ $\frac{1}{2}$ Ⓒ $\frac{2}{1}$

    Ⓑ $\frac{1}{3}$ Ⓓ $\frac{1}{1}$

5. **What fraction of the square is shaded?**

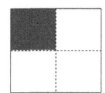

Ⓐ $\frac{1}{2}$

Ⓑ $\frac{1}{4}$

Ⓒ $\frac{1}{3}$

Ⓓ $\frac{3}{1}$

6. **What fraction of the square is NOT shaded?**

Ⓐ $\frac{1}{2}$

Ⓑ $\frac{1}{4}$

Ⓒ $\frac{3}{1}$

Ⓓ $\frac{3}{4}$

7. **What fraction of the circle is shaded?**

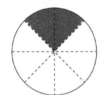

Ⓐ $\dfrac{1}{8}$

Ⓑ $\dfrac{2}{8}$

Ⓒ $\dfrac{2}{6}$

Ⓓ $\dfrac{6}{2}$

8. **What fraction of the circle is not shaded?**

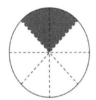

Ⓐ $\dfrac{6}{8}$

Ⓑ $\dfrac{7}{8}$

Ⓒ $\dfrac{2}{6}$

Ⓓ $\dfrac{6}{2}$

9. **What fraction of the circle is shaded?**

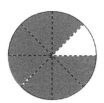

   Ⓐ $\dfrac{1}{8}$

   Ⓑ $\dfrac{1}{7}$

   Ⓒ $\dfrac{7}{1}$

   Ⓓ $\dfrac{7}{8}$

10. **What fraction of the circle is not shaded?**

   Ⓐ $\dfrac{1}{8}$

   Ⓑ $\dfrac{1}{7}$

   Ⓒ $\dfrac{7}{1}$

   Ⓓ $\dfrac{8}{1}$

11. What fraction of the rectangle is shaded?

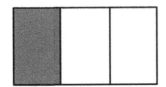

Ⓐ $\dfrac{1}{2}$

Ⓑ $\dfrac{1}{3}$

Ⓒ $\dfrac{2}{3}$

Ⓓ $\dfrac{2}{1}$

12. What fraction of the rectangle is not shaded?

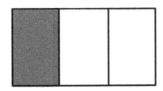

Ⓐ $\dfrac{1}{3}$

Ⓑ $\dfrac{1}{2}$

Ⓒ $\dfrac{2}{3}$

Ⓓ $\dfrac{2}{1}$

13. A pizza is cut into 12 equal slices. Eight slices are eaten. What fraction of the pizza is left?

Ⓐ $\dfrac{8}{12}$

Ⓑ $\dfrac{4}{8}$

Ⓒ $\dfrac{4}{12}$

Ⓓ $\dfrac{8}{4}$

14. The class has 20 children. Only half of the students brought their homework. How many students have their homework?

Ⓐ 20 students
Ⓑ 15 students
Ⓒ 10 students
Ⓓ 12 students

15. Meagan has 24 cupcakes. She gives a third of them to Micah. How many cupcakes does Micah have?

Ⓐ 8 cupcakes
Ⓑ 12 cupcakes
Ⓒ 3 cupcakes
Ⓓ 4 cupcakes

16. Which of the following fractions could apply to this figure? Complete the table by selecting yes or no.

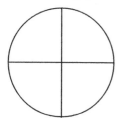

	Yes	No
1/8	○	○
1/4	○	○
1/3	○	○

17. What fraction does each figure show? Write your answers in the blank boxes.

Figure	Fraction
A 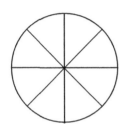	
B	
C	

18. Which of the following fractions could apply to this figure? Select all correct answers.

Ⓐ $\dfrac{1}{3}$

Ⓑ $\dfrac{1}{8}$

Ⓒ $\dfrac{1}{5}$

Ⓓ $\dfrac{8}{8}$

Chapter 4

Lesson 2: Fractions on the Number Line

You can scan the QR code given below or use the url to access additional EdSearch resources including videos and mobile apps related to *Fractions on the Number Line*.

 Fractions on the Number Line

URL	QR Code
http://www.lumoslearning.com/a/3nfa2	

1. **What fraction does the number line show?**

Ⓐ $\dfrac{1}{4}$

Ⓑ $\dfrac{1}{3}$

Ⓒ $\dfrac{3}{4}$

Ⓓ $\dfrac{4}{4}$

2. **What fraction does the number line show?**

Ⓐ $\dfrac{1}{2}$

Ⓑ $\dfrac{2}{2}$

Ⓒ $\dfrac{1}{3}$

Ⓓ $\dfrac{2}{3}$

3. **What fraction does the number line show?**

Ⓐ $\dfrac{2}{8}$

Ⓑ $\dfrac{3}{5}$

Ⓒ $\dfrac{3}{8}$

Ⓓ $\dfrac{4}{8}$

4. **What fraction does the number line show?**

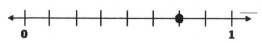

Ⓐ $\dfrac{3}{8}$

Ⓑ $\dfrac{6}{8}$

Ⓒ $\dfrac{5}{8}$

Ⓓ $\dfrac{4}{8}$

5. **What fraction does the number line show?**

Ⓐ $\dfrac{1}{6}$

Ⓑ $\dfrac{4}{6}$

Ⓒ $\dfrac{3}{6}$

Ⓓ $\dfrac{1}{5}$

6. **What fraction does the number line show?**

Ⓐ $\dfrac{2}{4}$

Ⓑ $\dfrac{2}{3}$

Ⓒ $\dfrac{1}{3}$

Ⓓ $\dfrac{1}{4}$

7. What fraction does the number line show?

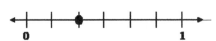

   (A) $\dfrac{1}{6}$

   (B) $\dfrac{3}{6}$

   (C) $\dfrac{2}{4}$

   (D) $\dfrac{2}{6}$

8. What fraction does the number line show?

   (A) $\dfrac{4}{8}$

   (B) $\dfrac{5}{8}$

   (C) $\dfrac{4}{4}$

   (D) $\dfrac{2}{8}$

9. What fraction does the number line show?

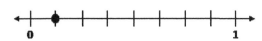

   (A) $\dfrac{2}{8}$

   (B) $\dfrac{2}{9}$

   (C) $\dfrac{1}{9}$

   (D) $\dfrac{1}{8}$

10. What fraction does the number line show

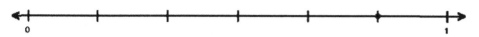

  Ⓐ $\dfrac{4}{6}$

  Ⓑ $\dfrac{5}{6}$

  Ⓒ $\dfrac{3}{6}$

  Ⓓ $\dfrac{1}{6}$

11. What fraction does the number line show?

  Ⓐ $\dfrac{2}{3}$

  Ⓑ $\dfrac{1}{3}$

  Ⓒ $\dfrac{3}{3}$

  Ⓓ $\dfrac{4}{3}$

12. What fraction does the number line show?

  Ⓐ $\dfrac{1}{4}$

  Ⓑ $\dfrac{2}{4}$

  Ⓒ $\dfrac{3}{4}$

  Ⓓ $\dfrac{4}{4}$

13. **What fraction does the number line show?**

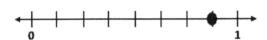

Ⓐ $\dfrac{8}{9}$

Ⓑ $\dfrac{7}{8}$

Ⓒ $\dfrac{2}{8}$

Ⓓ $\dfrac{5}{9}$

14. **What fraction does the number line show?**

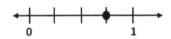

Ⓐ $\dfrac{1}{4}$

Ⓑ $\dfrac{3}{3}$

Ⓒ $\dfrac{2}{4}$

Ⓓ $\dfrac{3}{4}$

15. **What fraction does the number line show?**

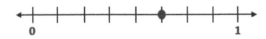

Ⓐ $\dfrac{7}{8}$

Ⓑ $\dfrac{6}{8}$

Ⓒ $\dfrac{5}{8}$

Ⓓ $\dfrac{5}{3}$

16. Which fractions does the number line show? Select all correct answers.

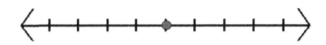

0   1

(A) $\dfrac{3}{6}$

(B) $\dfrac{1}{4}$

(C) $\dfrac{4}{8}$

(D) $\dfrac{1}{2}$

17. What fraction does the number line show? Write your answer in the box below.

0   1

18. Draw a number line and locate the fraction $\dfrac{5}{7}$ on it.

19. There are 3 number lines in the first column. Which fractions are represented by the dots on the number lines? For each number line, select the correct answer.

	4/4	8/9	5/8
(number line with dot, 0 to 1)	○	○	○
(number line with dot, 0 to 1)	○	○	○
(number line with dot, 0 to 1)	○	○	○

Chapter 4

Lesson 3: Comparing Fractions

You can scan the QR code given below or use the url to access additional EdSearch resources including videos and mobile apps related to *Comparing Fractions*.

 **Comparing Fractions**

URL	QR Code
http://www.lumoslearning.com/a/3nfa3	

1. Which of these sets has the fractions listed from least to greatest?

   Ⓐ $\dfrac{1}{6}, \dfrac{1}{4}, \dfrac{1}{3}, \dfrac{1}{2}$

   Ⓑ $\dfrac{1}{2}, \dfrac{1}{3}, \dfrac{1}{6}, \dfrac{1}{4}$

   Ⓒ $\dfrac{1}{3}, \dfrac{1}{4}, \dfrac{1}{2}, \dfrac{1}{6}$

   Ⓓ $\dfrac{1}{2}, \dfrac{1}{3}, \dfrac{1}{4}, \dfrac{1}{6}$

2. Which of these fractions would be found between $\dfrac{1}{2}$ and 1 on a number line?

   Ⓐ $\dfrac{1}{4}$

   Ⓑ $\dfrac{1}{3}$

   Ⓒ $\dfrac{5}{8}$

   Ⓓ $\dfrac{3}{1}$

3. Which of these fractions would be found between 0 an $\dfrac{1}{2}$ on a number line?

   Ⓐ $\dfrac{7}{8}$

   Ⓑ $\dfrac{3}{4}$

   Ⓒ $\dfrac{1}{4}$

   Ⓓ $\dfrac{5}{8}$

4. Which of these fractions would be found between 0 and $\frac{3}{4}$ on a number line?

   (A) $\frac{7}{8}$

   (B) $\frac{4}{8}$

   (C) $\frac{5}{6}$

   (D) $\frac{4}{4}$

5. Which of these fractions is less than $\frac{6}{8}$?

   (A) $\frac{1}{8}$

   (B) $\frac{7}{8}$

   (C) $\frac{9}{8}$

   (D) $\frac{8}{8}$

6. Answer the following: $\frac{1}{2}$ > _____?

   (A) $\frac{1}{4}$

   (B) $\frac{2}{3}$

   (C) $\frac{4}{8}$

   (D) $\frac{2}{2}$

7. Which is greater: $\frac{4}{8}$ or $\frac{1}{2}$?

   (A) $\frac{1}{2}$

   (B) $\frac{4}{8}$

   (C) They are equal.

   (D) There is not enough information given.

8. Which fraction is less: $\frac{1}{4}$ or $\frac{1}{8}$?

    Ⓐ $\frac{1}{4}$

    Ⓑ $\frac{1}{8}$

    Ⓒ They are equal.

    Ⓓ There is not enough information given.

9. Which fraction is less $\frac{4}{6}$ or $\frac{1}{6}$?

    Ⓐ $\frac{4}{6}$

    Ⓑ $\frac{1}{6}$

    Ⓒ They are equal.

    Ⓓ There is not enough information given.

10. If two fractions have the same denominator, the one with a(n) _____ numerator is the greater fraction.

    Ⓐ smaller
    Ⓑ greater
    Ⓒ even
    Ⓓ zero

11. Complete this number sentence: $\frac{4}{6}$ _____ $\frac{5}{6}$

    Ⓐ >
    Ⓑ <
    Ⓒ =
    Ⓓ There is not enough information given.

12. Complete this number sentence: $\frac{3}{8}$ _____ $\frac{5}{8}$

    Ⓐ >
    Ⓑ <
    Ⓒ =
    Ⓓ There is not enough information given.

13. Complete this number sentence: $\dfrac{2}{4}$ _____ $\dfrac{1}{2}$

    Ⓐ >
    Ⓑ <
    Ⓒ =
    Ⓓ There is not enough information given.

14. Complete this number sentence: $\dfrac{1}{2}$ _____ $\dfrac{1}{3}$

    Ⓐ >
    Ⓑ <
    Ⓒ =
    Ⓓ There is not enough information given.

15. To compare fractions with the same numerator, you need to look at the _____.

    Ⓐ numerators
    Ⓑ denominators
    Ⓒ factors of the numerator
    Ⓓ multiples of the denominator

16. Are the following fractions less than $\dfrac{3}{4}$? Select yes or no.

	Yes	No
$\dfrac{1}{4}$	◯	◯
$\dfrac{4}{4}$	◯	◯
$\dfrac{2}{4}$	◯	◯

17. Is Fraction #1 less than, greater than, or equal to Fraction #2? Write the correct symbol in the empty boxes.

Fraction #1	< = or >	Fraction #2
$\frac{2}{3}$		$\frac{1}{3}$
$\frac{4}{6}$		$\frac{5}{6}$
$\frac{8}{8}$		$\frac{5}{5}$
$\frac{3}{4}$		$\frac{1}{4}$

18. Which of the following fractions are greater than $\frac{2}{5}$? Select all correct answers.

Ⓐ $\frac{1}{5}$

Ⓑ $\frac{3}{5}$

Ⓒ $\frac{4}{5}$

Ⓓ $\frac{2}{5}$

19. Which of these fractions is greater than $\frac{5}{7}$? Circle the correct answer.

Ⓐ $\frac{1}{7}$

Ⓑ $\frac{2}{7}$

Ⓒ $\frac{4}{7}$

Ⓓ $\frac{6}{7}$

20. Which of the following fractions is the least?

$$\frac{6}{5}, \frac{6}{4}, \frac{6}{10}, \frac{6}{9}.$$

Write your answer in the box below.

_____

End of Number & Operations - Fractions

Chapter 5:
Measurement and Data

Lesson 1: Telling Time

You can scan the QR code given below or use the url to access additional EdSearch resources including videos and mobile apps related to *Telling Time*.

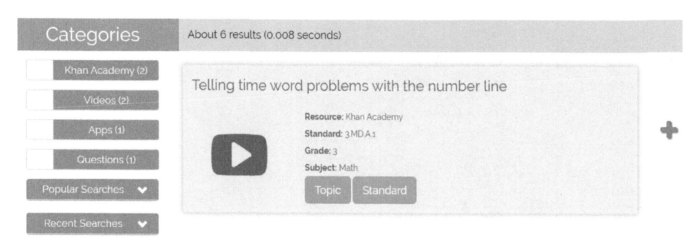

Categories | About 6 results (0.008 seconds)

Khan Academy (2)
Videos (2)
Apps (1)
Questions (1)
Popular Searches ⌄
Recent Searches ⌄

Telling time word problems with the number line

Resource: Khan Academy
Standard: 3.MD.A.1
Grade: 3
Subject: Math

Topic   Standard

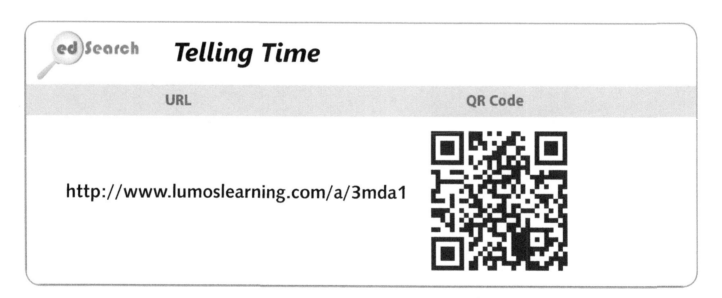

ed Search   *Telling Time*

URL	QR Code
http://www.lumoslearning.com/a/3mda1	

1. **What time does this clock show?**

Ⓐ 3:12
Ⓑ 2:17
Ⓒ 2:22
Ⓓ 2:03

2. **What time does this clock show?**

Ⓐ 5:42
Ⓑ 9:28
Ⓒ 6:47
Ⓓ 5:47

3. **What time does this clock show?**

Ⓐ 10:00
Ⓑ 12:50
Ⓒ 10:02
Ⓓ 9:41

4. **What time does this clock show?**

Ⓐ 12:39
Ⓑ 8:04
Ⓒ 1:38
Ⓓ 12:42

5. **On an analog clock, the shorter hand shows the _____ .**

Ⓐ minutes
Ⓑ hours
Ⓒ seconds
Ⓓ days

6. **On an analog clock, the longer hand shows the _____ .**

Ⓐ minutes
Ⓑ hours
Ⓒ days
Ⓓ seconds

7. **The clock currently shows:**

What time will it be in 8 minutes?

Ⓐ 1:38
Ⓑ 10:15
Ⓒ 10:10
Ⓓ 12:58

8. The clock currently shows:

What time will it be in 20 minutes?

Ⓐ 12:59
Ⓑ 1:09
Ⓒ 2:00
Ⓓ 8:24

9. The clock says:

What time was it 10 minutes ago?

Ⓐ 1:29
Ⓑ 12:29
Ⓒ 12:49
Ⓓ 1:09

10. Lucy started her test at 12:09 PM and finished at 12:58 PM. David started at 12:15 PM and ended at 1:03 PM. Who finished in a shorter amount of time?

Ⓐ Lucy
Ⓑ David
Ⓒ They both took the same amount of time.
Ⓓ There is not enough information given.

11. The Jamisons are on a road trip that will take 5 hours and 25 minutes. They have been driving for 3 hours and 41 minutes. How much longer do they need to travel before they reach their destination?

Ⓐ 1 hour, 13 minutes
Ⓑ 2 hours, 19 minutes
Ⓒ 1 hour, 44 minutes
Ⓓ 2 hours, 7 minutes

12. Rachel usually gets around 9 hours of sleep per night. She went to bed at 9:30 PM. About what time will she wake up?

   Ⓐ 8:30 AM
   Ⓑ 10:30 AM
   Ⓒ 6:30 AM
   Ⓓ 5:30 AM

13. A 45 minute long show ends at 12:20 PM. When did the show begin?

   Ⓐ 1:05 PM
   Ⓑ 11:35 AM
   Ⓒ 11:35 PM
   Ⓓ 11:45 AM

14. Mrs. James is giving her class a math test. She is allowing the students 40 minutes to finish the test. The test began at 10:22 AM. By what time must the test be finished?

   Ⓐ 10:42 AM
   Ⓑ 10:57 AM
   Ⓒ 11:02 AM
   Ⓓ 12:02 PM

15. The directions on a frozen pizza say to cook it for 25 minutes. Mr. Adams puts the frozen pizza in the oven at 5:43 PM. When will the pizza be done?

   Ⓐ 6:08 PM
   Ⓑ 6:18 PM
   Ⓒ 6:13 PM
   Ⓓ 5:58 PM

16. Which statements are true? Select all the correct answers.

   Ⓐ The minute hand points to 4
   Ⓑ The minute hand points to 6
   Ⓒ The hour hand points to 6
   Ⓓ The clock shows the time as 5:30

17. What time does this clock show? Write your answer in the box below.

18. Circle the clock that shows the time as 12:15

A   B   C

19. John starts working in the garden at 5:30 PM and finishes 40 minutes later. What time does the clock show when John finishes his work? Represent this on a number line.

20. The clocks in the first column show different times. For each clock in the first column, select the correct answer.

	9:42	11:58	2:03
clock showing ~11:59	○	○	○
clock showing ~12:08	○	○	○
clock showing ~8:47	○	○	○

Chapter 5

Lesson 2: Elapsed Time

You can scan the QR code given below or use the url to access additional EdSearch resources including videos and mobile apps related to *Elapsed Time*.

 Elapsed Time

URL	QR Code
http://www.lumoslearning.com/a/3mda1	

1. Cedric began reading his book at 9:12 AM. He finished at 10:02 AM. How long did it take him to read his book?

   Ⓐ 50 minutes
   Ⓑ 40 minutes
   Ⓒ 48 minutes
   Ⓓ 30 minutes

2. Samantha began eating her dinner at 7:11 PM and finished at 7:35 PM so that she could go to her room and play. How long did Samantha take to eat her dinner?

   Ⓐ 34 minutes
   Ⓑ 21 minutes
   Ⓒ 24 minutes
   Ⓓ 30 minutes

3. Tanya has after school tutoring from 3:00 PM until 3:25 PM. She began walking home at 3:31 PM and arrived at her house at 3:56 PM. How long did it take Tanya to walk home?

   Ⓐ 31 minutes
   Ⓑ 15 minutes
   Ⓒ 56 minutes
   Ⓓ 25 minutes

4. Doug loves to play video games. He started playing at 4:00 PM and did not finish until 5:27 PM. How long did Doug play video games?

   Ⓐ 1 hour and 37 minutes
   Ⓑ 1 hour and 27 minutes
   Ⓒ 27 minutes
   Ⓓ 2 hours and 27 minutes

5. Kelly has to clean her room before going to bed. She began cleaning her room at 6:12 PM. When she finished, it was 7:15 PM. How long did it take Kelly to clean her room?

   Ⓐ 57 minutes
   Ⓑ 53 minutes
   Ⓒ 1 hour and 3 minutes
   Ⓓ 1 hour and 15 minutes

6. Holly had a busy day. She attended a play from 7:06 PM until 8:13 PM. Then she went to dinner from 8:30 to 9:30 PM. How long did Holly attend the play?

   Ⓐ 57 minutes
   Ⓑ 2 hours and 27 minutes
   Ⓒ 46 minutes
   Ⓓ 1 hour and 7 minutes

7. Cara took her little brother to the park. They arrived at 3:11 PM and played until 4:37 PM. How long did Cara and her brother play at the park?

   Ⓐ 26 minutes
   Ⓑ 1 hour and 26 minutes
   Ⓒ 56 minutes
   Ⓓ 1 hour and 37 minutes

8. Arthur ran 5 miles. He began running at 8:19 AM and finished at 9:03 AM. How long did it take Arthur to run 5 miles?

   Ⓐ 44 minutes
   Ⓑ 45 minutes
   Ⓒ 40 minutes
   Ⓓ 54 minutes

9. Mr. Daniels wanted to see how fast he could wash the dishes. He began washing at 4:17 PM and finished at 4:32 PM. How long did it take Mr. Daniels to wash the dishes?

   Ⓐ 15 minutes
   Ⓑ 25 minutes
   Ⓒ 27 minutes
   Ⓓ 32 minutes

10. Sophia took a test that started at 3:28 PM. She finished the test at 4:11 PM. How long did it take Sophia to take her test?

    Ⓐ 37 minutes
    Ⓑ 47 minutes
    Ⓒ 33 minutes
    Ⓓ 43 minutes

11. Jonathan loves riding his bike, but he has to leave for football practice at 1:30 PM. If it is 1:11 PM now, how long does Jonathan have left to ride his bike before he has to leave for practice?

Ⓐ 9 minutes
Ⓑ 19 minutes
Ⓒ 21 minutes
Ⓓ 29 minutes

12. Mrs. Roberts loves to take a 20-minute nap on Saturdays. She was really tired when she went to sleep at 10:45 AM. She did not wake up until 11:25 AM. How long was Mrs. Roberts' long nap?

Ⓐ 40 minutes
Ⓑ 20 minutes
Ⓒ 60 minutes
Ⓓ 30 minutes

13. Spencer has to be at his piano lesson at noon. If it is now 11:29 AM, how long does Spencer have to get to his lesson?

Ⓐ 31 minutes
Ⓑ 1 minute
Ⓒ 29 minutes
Ⓓ 39 minutes

14. Look at the clocks below. How much time has elapsed between Clock A to Clock B?

Clock A	Clock B

Ⓐ 1 hour and 2 minutes
Ⓑ 1 hour and 12 minutes
Ⓒ 52 minutes
Ⓓ 42 minutes

15. Look at the clocks below. How much time has elapsed between Clock A to Clock B?

Clock A   Clock B

Ⓐ 52 minutes
Ⓑ 42 minutes
Ⓒ 12 minutes
Ⓓ 32 minutes

16. Tiana's daily schedule consists of classes that are 45 minutes long. The table shows what time some of her classes start. What time will each class end? Select the correct answer.

	9:05	10:55	12:15
History 10:10	○	○	○
Math 8:20	○	○	○
Gym 11:30	○	○	○

17. Jonas is taking a long road trip. He drives for one hour and then stops and rests for 15 minutes. He repeats this until the end of the trip. Complete the table to show his schedule.

Driving Start Time	Break Time
1:00	2:00
2:15	
3:30	4:30

18. How much time has passed? Select all the correct answers.

Ⓐ 1 hour
Ⓑ 90 minutes
Ⓒ 2 hours
Ⓓ 120 minutes

19. Observe the two clocks. How many minutes have passed between the time shown in the first clock to the time in the second clock. Write your answer in the box given below.

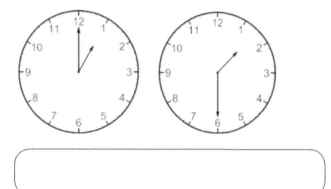

```


```

20. Tim went out to do some work. He left home at 11:30 AM and returned back at 3:45 PM. How long was he away from home? Circle the correct answer.

Ⓐ 3 hours and 15 minutes
Ⓑ 4 hours and 15 minutes
Ⓒ 3 hours and 45 minutes
Ⓓ 4 hours and 45 minutes

Chapter 5

Lesson 3: Liquid Volume & Mass

You can scan the QR code given below or use the url to access additional EdSearch resources including videos and mobile apps related to *Liquid Volume & Mass*.

 Liquid Volume & Mass

URL	QR Code
http://www.lumoslearning.com/a/3mda2	

1. "40 pounds" is printed at the bottom of a bag of sand. The number "40" is being used to _____ .

   Ⓐ count
   Ⓑ name
   Ⓒ locate
   Ⓓ measure

2. In the metric system, which is the best unit to measure the mass of a coffee table?

   Ⓐ Milliliters
   Ⓑ Kilograms
   Ⓒ Grams
   Ⓓ Liters

3. Which unit should be used to measure the amount of water in a small bowl?

   Ⓐ Cups
   Ⓑ Gallons
   Ⓒ Inches
   Ⓓ Tons

4. Which unit in the customary system is best suited to measure the weight of a coffee table?

   Ⓐ Gallons
   Ⓑ Pounds
   Ⓒ Quarts
   Ⓓ Ounces

5. Which of these units could be used to measure the capacity of a container?

   Ⓐ pints
   Ⓑ feet
   Ⓒ pounds
   Ⓓ millimeters

6. Which of these is a unit of mass?

   Ⓐ liter
   Ⓑ meter
   Ⓒ gram
   Ⓓ degree

7. Which of these units has the greatest capacity?

    Ⓐ gallon
    Ⓑ pint
    Ⓒ cup
    Ⓓ quart

8. Which of these might be the weight of an average sized 8 year-old child?

    Ⓐ 15 pounds
    Ⓑ 30 pounds
    Ⓒ 65 pounds
    Ⓓ 150 pounds

9. Volume is measured in _____ units.

    Ⓐ cubic
    Ⓑ liters
    Ⓒ square
    Ⓓ box

10. What is an appropriate unit to measure the weight of a dog?

    Ⓐ tons
    Ⓑ pounds
    Ⓒ inches
    Ⓓ gallons

11. What is an appropriate unit to measure the amount of water in a swimming pool?

    Ⓐ teaspoons
    Ⓑ cups
    Ⓒ gallons
    Ⓓ inches

12. What is an appropriate unit to measure the distance across a city?

    Ⓐ centimeters
    Ⓑ feet
    Ⓒ inches
    Ⓓ miles

13. **What is an appropriate unit to measure the amount of salt in a cupcake recipe?**

Ⓐ teaspoons
Ⓑ gallons
Ⓒ miles
Ⓓ kilograms

14. **Which unit is the largest?**

Ⓐ mile
Ⓑ centimeter
Ⓒ foot
Ⓓ inch

15. **Which unit is the smallest?**

Ⓐ kilometer
Ⓑ centimeter
Ⓒ millimeter
Ⓓ inch

16. **Which units of measurement could be used to measure how much water a pot can hold? Select all the correct answers.**

Ⓐ quarts
Ⓑ centimeter
Ⓒ liters
Ⓓ miles

17. **Observe the figure given. How many cups of liquid does this measuring cup hold? Write your answer in the box given below.**

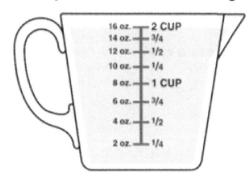

18. Circle the tool that should be used to measure a small amount of sugar.

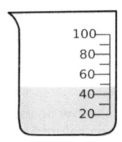

19. There are 8 water coolers in a school. Each water cooler holds 7 liters of water. All the water coolers were filled up in the morning. In the evening 5 liters of water remained. How much water was consumed? Explain how you got the answer in the box below.

Chapter 5

Lesson 4: Graphs

You can scan the QR code given below or use the url to access additional EdSearch resources including videos and mobile apps related to *Graphs*.

 **Graphs**

URL	QR Code
http://www.lumoslearning.com/a/3mdb3	

1.

Class Survey Should there be a field trip?		
	Yes	**No**
Mr. A's class	ЦНТ ЦНТ IIII	ЦНТ II
Mr. B's class	ЦНТ ЦНТ ЦНТ	ЦНТ ЦНТ III
Mr. C's class	ЦНТ ЦНТ I	ЦНТ ЦНТ I
Mr. D's class	ЦНТ ЦНТ II	ЦНТ ЦНТ

Four 3rd grade classes in Hill Elementary School were surveyed to find out if they wanted to go on a field trip at the end of the school year. The tally table above was used to record the votes.

How many kids voted "Yes" in Mrs. B's class?

Ⓐ 28 kids
Ⓑ 15 kids
Ⓒ 13 kids
Ⓓ 23 kids

2.

Should there be a field trip?		
	Yes	**No**
Mr. A's class	14	7
Mr. B's class	15	13
Mr. C's class	11	11
Mr. D's class	12	10
Total	52	41

Four 3rd grade classes in Hill Elementary School were surveyed to find out if they wanted to go on a field trip at the end of the school year. The table above shows the results of the survey.

How many kids voted "Yes" in Mr. A's class?

Ⓐ 7 kids
Ⓑ 15 kids
Ⓒ 14 kids
Ⓓ 21 kids

3.

Should there be a field trip?		
	Yes	No
Mr. A's class	14	7
Mr. B's class	15	13
Mr. C's class	11	11
Mr. D's class	12	10
Total	52	41

Four 3rd grade classes in Hill Elementary School were surveyed to find out if they wanted to go on a field trip at the end of the school year. The table above shows the results of the survey.
How many kids altogether voted "No" for the field trip?

Ⓐ 82 kids
Ⓑ 11 kids
Ⓒ 52 kids
Ⓓ 41 kids

4. The students in Mr. Donovan's class were surveyed to find out their favorite school subjects. The results are shown in the pictograph. Use the pictograph to answer the following question:
How many students chose either science or math?

Our Favorite Subjects

Math	○○○○
Reading	○○
Science	○○○
History	○
Other	○○

Key: ○ = 2 votes

Ⓐ 6 students
Ⓑ 7 students
Ⓒ 14 students
Ⓓ 2 students

5.

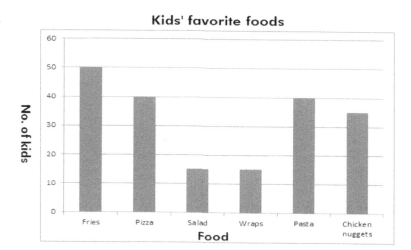

The third graders in Valley Elementary School were asked to pick their favorite food from 6 choices. The results are shown in the bar graph.

Which food was the favorite of the most children?

Ⓐ Pizza
Ⓑ Pasta
Ⓒ Fries
Ⓓ Salad

6.

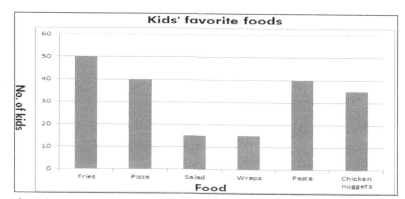

The third graders in Valley Elementary School were asked to pick their favorite food from 6 choices. The results are shown in the bar graph.

What are the 2 foods that kids like the least?

Ⓐ Fries and Pizza
Ⓑ Pizza and Pasta
Ⓒ Pasta and Chicken Nuggets
Ⓓ Salad and Wraps

7.

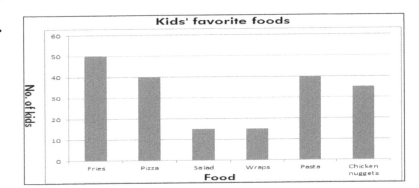

The third graders in Valley Elementary School were asked to pick their favorite food from 6 choices. The results are shown in the bar graph.

How many kids chose pasta?

Ⓐ 50 kids
Ⓑ 15 kids
Ⓒ 40 kids
Ⓓ 35 kids

8.

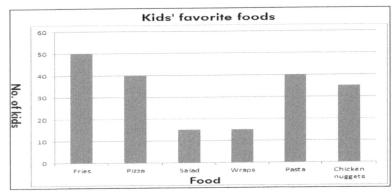

The third graders in Valley Elementary School were asked to pick their favorite food from 6 choices. The results are shown in the bar graph.

How many more kids prefer fries than pizza?

Ⓐ 50 more kids
Ⓑ 10 more kids
Ⓒ 1 more kid
Ⓓ 15 more kids

9.

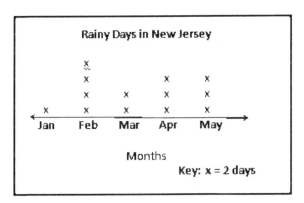

The line plot shows the number of days it rained in New Jersey from January through May. What is the title of the above graph?

Ⓐ Line plot
Ⓑ Rainy Days in New Jersey
Ⓒ Months
Ⓓ 2 days

10.

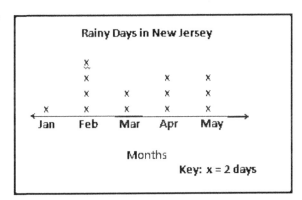

Which of the following statements about the above graph is true?

Ⓐ The graph shows New Jersey's monthly rainy days from January through May.
Ⓑ The graph shows the amount of rain accumulated each day.
Ⓒ The graph shows the average temperature during the 5 month period.
Ⓓ The graph shows New Jersey's total number of rainy days for the year.

11.

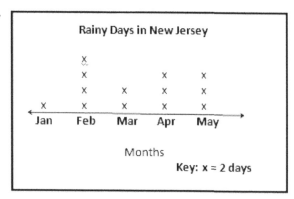

According to the graph, which month had the most rainy days?

Ⓐ March
Ⓑ February
Ⓒ January
Ⓓ April

12. A survey was taken to find out the favorite sports of third graders in a particular class. The results are shown in the tally table. Use the table to answer the following question: How many students were surveyed altogether?

Our Favorite Sports

Soccer	𝗡𝗛𝗟 𝙸
Tennis	𝙸𝙸𝙸𝙸
Baseball	𝗡𝗛𝗟 𝙸𝙸𝙸
Hockey	𝙸𝙸𝙸𝙸
Other	𝙸𝙸𝙸

Ⓐ 20 students
Ⓑ 25 students
Ⓒ 24 students
Ⓓ 27 students

13. A survey was taken to find out the favorite sports of third graders in a particular class. The results are shown in the tally table. Use the table to answer the following question: How many more students chose soccer than chose hockey?

Our Favorite Sports

Soccer	ⵜⵜ |
Tennis	||||
Baseball	ⵜⵜ |||
Hockey	||||
Other	|||

Ⓐ **6 students**
Ⓑ **4 students**
Ⓒ **2 students**
Ⓓ **3 students**

14. A survey was taken to find out the favorite sports of third graders in a particular class. The results are shown in the tally table. Use the table to answer the following question: How many students chose baseball as their favorite sport?

Our Favorite Sports

Soccer	ⵜⵜ |
Tennis	||||
Baseball	ⵜⵜ |||
Hockey	||||
Other	|||

Ⓐ **9 students**
Ⓑ **8 students**
Ⓒ **3 students**
Ⓓ **6 students**

15. A survey was taken to find out the favorite sports of third graders in a particular class. The results are shown in the tally table. Use the table to answer the following question: Which two sports were chosen by the same number of students?

Our Favorite Sports

Soccer	ⅢⅠ Ⅰ
Tennis	ⅠⅠⅠⅠ
Baseball	ⅢⅠ ⅠⅠⅠ
Hockey	ⅠⅠⅠⅠ
Other	ⅠⅠⅠ

Ⓐ soccer and tennis
Ⓑ soccer and baseball
Ⓒ hockey and soccer
Ⓓ hockey and tennis

16. Mrs. Brown's class voted on which day they will have a class party. Look at the graph. Each figure represents 1 student. Match the correct answers to the number of votes.

Student Party Day Votes

Monday   Tuesday   Wednesday   Thursday   Friday

	5	2	4
Total votes for Friday	○	○	○
Total votes for Wednesday	○	○	○
Total votes for Monday	○	○	○

17. Coach Dennis is creating a graph. He wants to purchase bats for his team. He needs to purchase 8 bats. He needs half of the bats to be made of wood. The other half will be made of aluminum. He decides that he will purchase 3 more bats made of plastic as well. Complete the table by filling in the correct answers.

Type of Bat	Number of Bats Needed
Wood	
Aluminum	
Plastic	

18. Vicki is planting a flower garden. The graph above shows the number of flowers to be planted in the garden. Which of the following statements are true? Select all the correct answers.

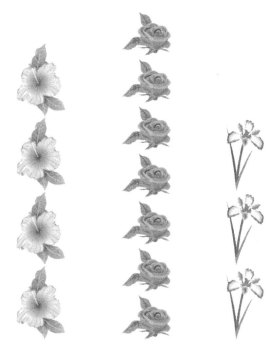

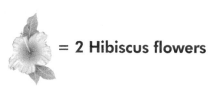 = 2 Hibiscus flowers

 = 2 Rose flowers

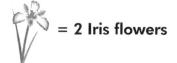 = 2 Iris flowers

Ⓐ The count of Rose flowers is 14
Ⓑ The Count of Rose flowers is 7
Ⓒ The count of Hibiscus flowers is 4
Ⓓ The count of Iris flowers is 6

19. Find the total number of each coin. Use the tally chart to draw a bar graph.

Coins in John's Piggy Bank		
Coin	Tally	Number of Coins
Penny	|||| |||| |||| |||| ||	
Nickel	|||| |||| |||| |||	
Dime	|||| |||| ||||	
Quarter	|||| |||| ||||		

20. From the Venn Diagram given below, represent the number of people who only own cats as pet to the number of people who own only dogs as a pet in the form of a fraction $\frac{a}{b}$ (ratio of number of people owning cats to dogs)

Pets We Have
Cat   Dog

Liz   Ryan
     Tim
Carly Ann   Joe

          Will

Chapter 5

Lesson 5: Measuring Length

You can scan the QR code given below or use the url to access additional EdSearch resources including videos and mobile apps related to *Measuring Length*.

 Measuring Length

URL	QR Code
http://www.lumoslearning.com/a/3mdb4	

1. Which of these units is part of the metric system?

    Ⓐ Foot
    Ⓑ Mile
    Ⓒ Kilometer
    Ⓓ Yard

2. Which metric unit is closest in length to one yard?

    Ⓐ decimeter
    Ⓑ meter
    Ⓒ millimeter
    Ⓓ kilometer

3. Which of these is the best estimate for the length of a table?

    Ⓐ 2 decimeters
    Ⓑ 2 centimeters
    Ⓒ 2 meters
    Ⓓ 2 kilometers

4. What unit should you use to measure the length of a book?

    Ⓐ Kilometers
    Ⓑ Meters
    Ⓒ Centimeters
    Ⓓ Grams

5. About how long is a new pencil?

    Ⓐ 8 inches
    Ⓑ 8 feet
    Ⓒ 8 yards
    Ⓓ 8 miles

6. Which of these is the best estimate for the length of a football?

    Ⓐ 1 foot
    Ⓑ 2 feet
    Ⓒ 6 feet
    Ⓓ 4 feet

7. Complete the following statement.
   The length of a football field is _____.

   Ⓐ less than one meter
   Ⓑ greater than one meter
   Ⓒ about one meter
   Ⓓ impossible to measure

8. Complete the following statement.
   An adult's pointer finger is about one _____ wide.

   Ⓐ meter
   Ⓑ kilometer
   Ⓒ millimeter
   Ⓓ centimeter

9. Complete the following statement.
   The distance between two cities would most likely be measured in _____.

   Ⓐ hours
   Ⓑ miles
   Ⓒ yards
   Ⓓ square inches

10. A ribbon is 25 centimeters long. About how many inches long is it?

    Ⓐ 2
    Ⓑ 25
    Ⓒ 10
    Ⓓ 50

11. _____

How long is this object?

Ⓐ 4 inches
Ⓑ 8 inches
Ⓒ 10 inches
Ⓓ 12 inches

12. ▬▬▬▬

How long is this object?

Ⓐ 2 inches
Ⓑ 5 inches
Ⓒ 3 inches
Ⓓ 1 inch

13.

How long is this object?

Ⓐ 6 inches
Ⓑ 5 and a half inches
Ⓒ 6 and a half inches
Ⓓ 7 inches

14. Which statement is correct?

Ⓐ 1 inch > 1 mile
Ⓑ 1 inch > 1 centimeter
Ⓒ 1 foot < 1 inch
Ⓓ 1 mile < 1 foot

15. Which is correct?

Ⓐ 12 inches > 1 foot
Ⓑ 12 inches < 1 foot
Ⓒ 12 inches = 1 foot
Ⓓ 9 inches = 1 foot

16. Which of the following could be measured with a ruler? Select all correct answers.

Ⓐ water in a bowl
Ⓑ a football field
Ⓒ a carrot
Ⓓ a crayon

17. Observe the figure. How long is the pencil when measured in inches?

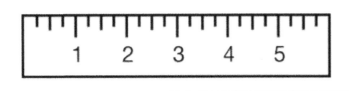

18. Fill in the correct answer in the blanks shown in the table.

Measurement in inches	Measurement in half inches	Measurement in quarter inches
$3\frac{1}{2}$ inches	7 half inches	14 quarter inches
$2\frac{1}{2}$ inches		
	11 half inches	
		26 quarter inches

19. Use the line plot to answer the questions given in the first column.

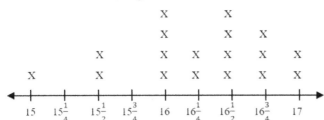

Lengths of Fish

Instruction:
X = 2 fishes

	4	6	8
How many fish are $16\frac{1}{2}$ inches long?	○	○	○
How many more fish are 16 inches long than 17 inches?	○	○	○
How many fish are less than $15\frac{3}{4}$ inches long?	○	○	○

Chapter 5

Lesson 6: Area

You can scan the QR code given below or use the url to access additional EdSearch resources including videos and mobile apps related to *Area*.

 **Area**

URL	QR Code
http://www.lumoslearning.com/a/3mdc6	

1. The area of a plane figure is measured in _____ units.

   Ⓐ cubic
   Ⓑ meter
   Ⓒ square
   Ⓓ box

2. Which of these objects has an area of about 1 square inch?

   Ⓐ a sheet of writing paper
   Ⓑ a beach towel
   Ⓒ a dollar bill
   Ⓓ a postage stamp

3. Mr. Parker wants to cover a mural with cloth. The mural is 12 inches long and 20 inches wide. How many square inches of cloth does Mr. Parker need?

   Ⓐ 240 square inches
   Ⓑ 32 square inches
   Ⓒ 120 square inches
   Ⓓ 220 square inches

4.

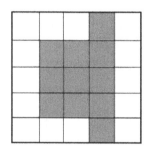

☐ = 1 Square Unit

   What is the area of the shaded region?

   Ⓐ 10 square units
   Ⓑ 8 square units
   Ⓒ 11 square units
   Ⓓ 15 square units

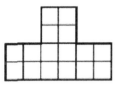

5. Find the area of this figure.

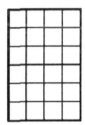

☐ =1 Square Unit

Ⓐ 22 square units
Ⓑ 20 square units
Ⓒ 18 square units
Ⓓ 16 square units

6. Find the area of this figure.

☐ =1 Square Unit

Ⓐ 22 square units
Ⓑ 20 square units
Ⓒ 24 square units
Ⓓ 28 square units

7. Find the area of the shaded region.

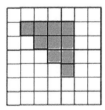

☐ =1 Square Unit

Ⓐ 11 square units
Ⓑ 10 square units
Ⓒ 16 square units
Ⓓ 9 square units

8. Find the area of the shaded region.

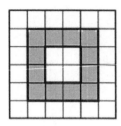

☐ =1 Square Unit

Ⓐ 16 square units
Ⓑ 12 square units
Ⓒ 10 square units
Ⓓ 11 square units

9. Find the area of the shaded region.

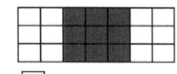

Key: ☐ =1 Square Unit

Ⓐ 5 square units
Ⓑ 6 square units
Ⓒ 8 square units
Ⓓ 9 square units

10. The area of Karen's rectangular room is 72 sq. ft. If the length of the room is 8 ft. What is its width? Drag your answer into the box. Find the area of the shaded region.

Ⓐ 8 ft.
Ⓑ 6 ft.
Ⓒ 7 ft.
Ⓓ 9 ft.

11. Can these items be measured in square units? Select yes or no.

	Yes	No
Window panes		
A ball		
Bathroom tile		
A banana		

12. Find the area of the shaded region in each figure. Each box is 1 square unit. Write your answers in the blank boxes in the table.

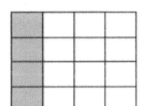

Figure A

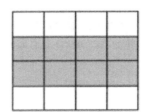

Figure B

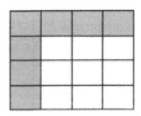

Figure C

Figure	Area
Figure A	
Figure B	
Figure C	

13. Find the area of the figure. Write your answer in the box given below.

6 feet

9 feet

square feet

14. Which of the following are possible ways to find the area of this figure? Each box is 1 square unit. Select all correct answers.

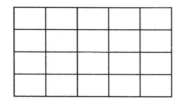

    Ⓐ Count the total number of square units
    Ⓑ Multiplying the length by the width of the figure
    Ⓒ Multiplying the number of square units by 2
    Ⓓ Subtracting the length of the figure from the width

15. The area of a rectangle A is 75 sq. cm. The area of square B is one third the area of the rectangle A. What is the side length of the square B? Circle the correct answer.

    Ⓐ 7 cm
    Ⓑ 5 cm
    Ⓒ 4 cm
    Ⓓ 6 cm

Chapter 5

Lesson 7: Relating Area to Addition & Multiplication

You can scan the QR code given below or use the url to access additional EdSearch resources including videos and mobile apps related to *Relating Area to Addition & Multiplication*.

ed Search *Relating Area to Addition & Multiplication*

URL	QR Code
http://www.lumoslearning.com/a/3mdc7	

1. Find the area of the object below.

3 feet

29 feet

(A) 87 square feet
(B) 32 square feet
(C) 64 square feet
(D) 128 square feet

2. Find the area of the object below.

12 yards

15 yards

(A) 108 square yards
(B) 54 square yards
(C) 27 square yards
(D) 180 square yards

3. How could the area of this figure be calculated?

33 inches

63 inches

(A) Multiply 63 x 33 x 63 x 33
(B) Add 63 + 33 + 63 + 33
(C) Multiply 63 x 33
(D) Multiply 2 x 63 x 33

4. **Find the area of the object below.**

5 meters

10 meters

Ⓐ 75 square meters
Ⓑ 50 square meters
Ⓒ 15 square meters
Ⓓ 30 square meters

5. **Find the area of the object below.**

16 yards

11 yards

Ⓐ 176 square yards
Ⓑ 27 square yards
Ⓒ 54 square yards
Ⓓ 2,916 square yards

6. **Find the area of the object below.**

3 inches

2 inches + 3 inches

Ⓐ 18 square inches
Ⓑ 15 square inches
Ⓒ 9 square inches
Ⓓ 6 square inches

7. **Find the area of the object below.**

7 feet

2 feet + 1 foot

Ⓐ 16 square feet
Ⓑ 14 square feet
Ⓒ 9 square feet
Ⓓ 21 square feet

8. Find the area of the object below.

12 meters

4 meters + 3 meters

Ⓐ 84 square meters
Ⓑ 48 square meters
Ⓒ 36 square meters
Ⓓ 72 square meters

9. Find the area of the object below.

5 inches

5 inches + 2 inches

Ⓐ 12 square inches
Ⓑ 10 square inches
Ⓒ 25 square inches
Ⓓ 35 square inches

10. Find the area of the object below.

13 yards

7 yards+7 yards

Ⓐ 84 square yards
Ⓑ 182 square yards
Ⓒ 26 square yards
Ⓓ 19 square yards

11. The city wants to plant grass in a park. The park is 20 feet by 50 feet. How much grass will they need to cover the entire park?

Ⓐ 100 square feet
Ⓑ 500 square feet
Ⓒ 1,000 square feet
Ⓓ 1,100 square feet

12. Brenda wants to purchase a rug for her room. Her room is a rectangle that measures 7 yards by 6 yards. What is the area of her room?

    Ⓐ 42 square yards
    Ⓑ 48 square yards
    Ⓒ 36 square yards
    Ⓓ 26 square yards

13. Joan wants to cover her backyard with flowers. If her backyard is 30 feet long and 20 feet wide, what is the area that needs to be covered in flowers?

    Ⓐ 60 square feet
    Ⓑ 500 square feet
    Ⓒ 600 square feet
    Ⓓ 100 square feet

14. Bethany decided to paint the four walls in her room. If each wall measures 20 feet by 10 feet, how many total square feet will she need to paint?

    Ⓐ 400 square feet
    Ⓑ 200 square feet
    Ⓒ 800 square feet
    Ⓓ 600 square feet

15. Seth wants to cover his table top with a piece of fabric. His table is 2 meters long and 4 meters wide. How much fabric does Seth need?

    Ⓐ 6 square meters
    Ⓑ 10 square meters
    Ⓒ 8 square meters
    Ⓓ 16 square meters

Name _____   Date _____

Chapter 5

Lesson 8: Perimeter

You can scan the QR code given below or use the url to access additional EdSearch resources including videos and mobile apps related to *Perimeter*.

 Perimeter

URL	QR Code
http://www.lumoslearning.com/a/3mdd8	

Name _____   Date _____

1. What is meant by the "perimeter" of a shape?

   Ⓐ The distance from the center of a plane figure to its edge
   Ⓑ The distance from one corner of a plane figure to an opposite corner
   Ⓒ The distance around the outside of a plane figure
   Ⓓ The amount of space covered by a plane figure

2. Complete the following statement.
   Two measurements associated with plane figures are _____.

   Ⓐ perimeter and volume
   Ⓑ perimeter and area
   Ⓒ volume and area
   Ⓓ weight and volume

3.

   This rectangle is 4 units long and one unit wide. What is its perimeter?

   Ⓐ 10 units
   Ⓑ 4 units
   Ⓒ 5 units
   Ⓓ 8 units

4.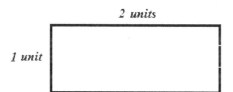

   What is the perimeter of the rectangle?

   Ⓐ 5 units
   Ⓑ 6 units
   Ⓒ 3 units
   Ⓓ 2 units

5.

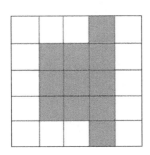

= 1 Square Unit

What is the perimeter of the shaded region in the above figure?

Ⓐ 16 units
Ⓑ 15 units
Ⓒ 11 units
Ⓓ 10 units

6. The perimeter of this rhombus is 20 units. How long is each of its sides?

Ⓐ 4 units
Ⓑ 10 units
Ⓒ 5 units
Ⓓ This cannot be determined.

7. Each side of this rhombus measures 3 centimeters. What is its perimeter?

Ⓐ 3 centimeters
Ⓑ 12 centimeters
Ⓒ 9 centimeters
Ⓓ 6 centimeters

Name _____   Date _____

8. This square has a perimeter of 80 units. How long is each of its sides?

Ⓐ 8 units
Ⓑ 10 units
Ⓒ 20 units
Ⓓ 40 units

9. Find the perimeter of this figure.

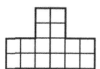

□ = 1 Square Unit

Ⓐ 20 units
Ⓑ 18 units
Ⓒ 16 units
Ⓓ 22 units

10. Joan wants to cover the outside border of her backyard with flowers. If her backyard is 30 feet long and 15 feet wide, how many feet of flowers does she need to plant?

Ⓐ 450 feet
Ⓑ 90 feet
Ⓒ 60 feet
Ⓓ 30 feet

11. Find the perimeter of this figure.

□ = 1 Square Unit

Ⓐ 20 units
Ⓑ 18 units
Ⓒ 24 units
Ⓓ 22 units

12. Brenda wants to place rope around a large field in order to play a game. The field is a rectangle that measures 23 yards by 32 yards. How much rope does Brenda need?

Ⓐ 64 yards
Ⓑ 736 yards
Ⓒ 110 yards
Ⓓ 55 yards

13. Find the perimeter of the following object.

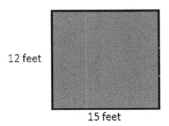

12 feet

15 feet

Ⓐ 54 feet
Ⓑ 27 feet
Ⓒ 58 feet
Ⓓ 180 feet

14. Find the perimeter of the following object.

16 feet

11 feet

Ⓐ 42 feet
Ⓑ 176 feet
Ⓒ 27 feet
Ⓓ 54 feet

15. Find the perimeter of the shaded region.

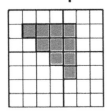

= 1 Square Unit

Ⓐ 10 units
Ⓑ 13 units
Ⓒ 15 units
Ⓓ 16 units

16. Find the perimeter of the following object.

3 feet

29 feet

Ⓐ 32 feet
Ⓑ 87 feet
Ⓒ 172 feet
Ⓓ 64 feet

17. The city is building a fence around a park. The park is 20 feet by 50 feet. How many feet of fencing do they need?

20 feet

50 feet

Ⓐ 100 feet
Ⓑ 120 feet
Ⓒ 140 feet
Ⓓ 70 feet

18. Find the perimeter of the following object.

33 inches

53 inches

Ⓐ 86 inches
Ⓑ 172 inches
Ⓒ 1,749 inches
Ⓓ 50 inches

19. Find the perimeter of the following object.

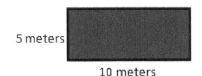

5 meters

10 meters

Ⓐ 15 meters
Ⓑ 25 meters
Ⓒ 30 meters
Ⓓ 50 meters

20. The perimeter of the following object is 16 feet. Find the length of the missing side.

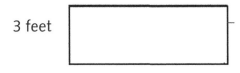

3 feet

X

Ⓐ x = 5 feet
Ⓑ x = 10 feet
Ⓒ x = 13 feet
Ⓓ x = 6 feet

21. The perimeter of the following object is 20 feet. Find the length of the missing side.

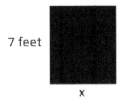

7 feet

x

Ⓐ x = 3 feet
Ⓑ x = 6 feet
Ⓒ x = 13 feet
Ⓓ x = 7 feet

22. The city is building a fence around a park. The park is 20 feet by 50 feet. If they only want the fence on 3 sides, what is the least amount of fencing they could buy?

Ⓐ 140 feet
Ⓑ 100 feet
Ⓒ 120 feet
Ⓓ 90 feet

23. The perimeter of the following object is 38 feet. Find the length of the missing side.

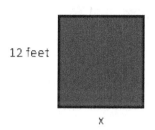

12 feet

x

(A) x = 17 feet
(B) x = 12 feet
(C) x = 7 feet
(D) x = 26 feet

24. The perimeter of the following object is 24 inches. Find the length of the missing side.

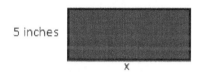

5 inches

x

(A) x = 19 inches
(B) x = 7 inches
(C) x = 9 inches
(D) x = 12 inches

25. The perimeter of the following object is 54 yards. Find the length of the missing side.

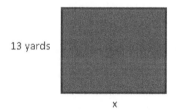

13 yards

x

(A) x = 28 yards
(B) x = 14 yards
(C) x = 41 yards
(D) x = 27 yards

26. Which of the following statements are true? Select all correct answers.

Ⓐ The perimeter is the distance around the outside of a plane figure.
Ⓑ The perimeter is the center of a circle.
Ⓒ The perimeter can be found by adding the angles of a triangle.
Ⓓ The perimeter can be found by adding the length of a figure's sides.

27. What is the perimeter of the rectangle shown in figure below? Write your answer in the box given

3 units

6 units

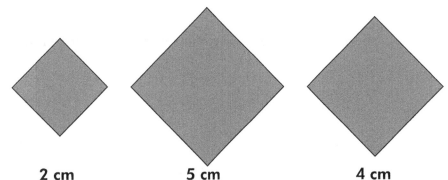

28. Circle the rhombus that has a perimeter of 8.0 cm.

2 cm   5 cm   4 cm

29. John draws a regular hexagon. Each side measures 8 centimeters. He also draws a regular octagon. Each side of the octagon measures 7 centimeters. Which shape has a greater perimeter? How did you arrive at the answer?

30. The perimeters of the rectangles are given in the first column. For each perimeter, select the possible areas of the rectangles.
Note that for each perimeter, more than one option may be correct.
Instruction: Assume that the length and the width of the rectangles are whole numbers.

	15 sq. cm.	10 sq. cm.	12 sq. cm.
Perimeter = 16 cm	☐	☐	☐
Perimeter = 14 cm	☐	☐	☐
Perimeter = 22 cm	☐	☐	☐

End of Measurement & Data

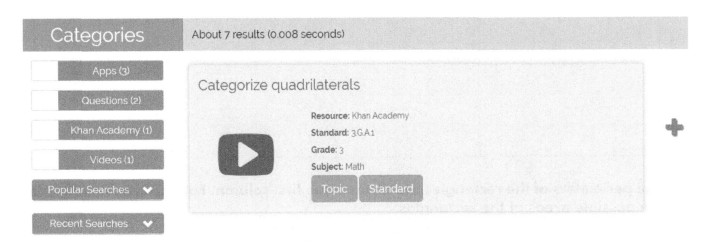
Chapter 6: Geometry

Lesson 1: 2-Dimensional Shapes

You can scan the QR code given below or use the url to access additional EdSearch resources including videos and mobile apps related to *2-Dimensional Shapes*.

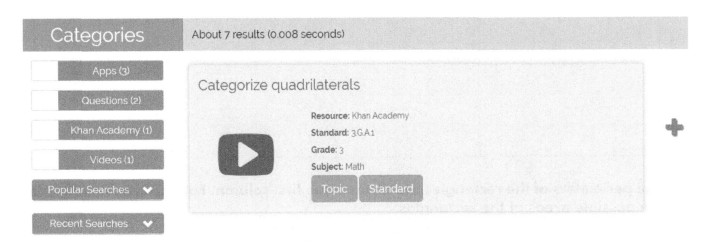

Categories	About 7 results (0.008 seconds)
Apps (3)	**Categorize quadrilaterals**
Questions (2)	**Resource:** Khan Academy
Khan Academy (1)	**Standard:** 3.G.A.1
Videos (1)	**Grade:** 3
Popular Searches ⌄	**Subject:** Math
Recent Searches ⌄	Topic Standard

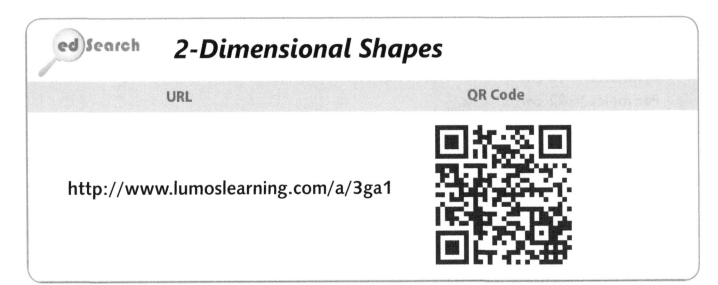

ed)Search *2-Dimensional Shapes*

URL	QR Code
http://www.lumoslearning.com/a/3ga1	

1. Fill in the blank with the correct term.
   Closed, plane figures that have straight sides are called _____ .

   Ⓐ parallelograms
   Ⓑ line segments
   Ⓒ polygons
   Ⓓ squares

2. Which of the following shapes is not a polygon?

   Ⓐ Square
   Ⓑ Hexagon
   Ⓒ Circle
   Ⓓ Pentagon

3. Complete this statement.
   A rectangle must have _____ .

   Ⓐ four right angles
   Ⓑ four straight angles
   Ⓒ four obtuse angles
   Ⓓ four acute angles

4. How many sides does a trapezoid have?

   Ⓐ 4
   Ⓑ 8
   Ⓒ 6
   Ⓓ 10

5. Complete the following statement.
   A square is always a _____ .

   Ⓐ rhombus
   Ⓑ parallelogram
   Ⓒ rectangle
   Ⓓ All of the above

6. Which of these statements is true?

   Ⓐ A square and a triangle have the same number of angles.
   Ⓑ A triangle has more angles than a square.
   Ⓒ A square has more angles than a triangle.
   Ⓓ A square and a triangle each have no angles.

7. **Which of these statements is true?**

   Ⓐ A rectangle has more sides than a trapezoid.
   Ⓑ A parallelogram and a trapezoid have the same number of sides.
   Ⓒ A triangle has more sides than a trapezoid.
   Ⓓ A triangle has more sides than a square.

8. **Complete this statement.**
   A trapezoid must have _____.

   Ⓐ two acute angles
   Ⓑ two right angles
   Ⓒ one pair of parallel sides
   Ⓓ two pairs of parallel sides

9. **Complete the following statement.**
   Squares, rectangles, rhombi and trapezoids are all _____.

   Ⓐ triangles
   Ⓑ quadrilaterals
   Ⓒ angles
   Ⓓ round

10. **Which of these shapes is a quadrilateral?**

    Ⓐ circle
    Ⓑ triangle
    Ⓒ rectangle
    Ⓓ pentagon

11. **Which of these shapes is NOT a quadrilateral?**

    Ⓐ square
    Ⓑ trapezoid
    Ⓒ rectangle
    Ⓓ triangle

12. **Name the figure shown below.**

    Ⓐ Trapezoid
    Ⓑ Square
    Ⓒ Pentagon
    Ⓓ Rhombus

13. Name the object shown below.

Ⓐ **Rectangle**
Ⓑ **Parallelogram**
Ⓒ **Trapezoid**
Ⓓ **Rhombus**

14. The figure shown below is a _____ .

Ⓐ parallelogram
Ⓑ rectangle
Ⓒ quadrilateral
Ⓓ All of the above

15. The figure below is a _____ .

Ⓐ triangle
Ⓑ square
Ⓒ rhombus
Ⓓ trapezoid

16. Are these figures quadrilaterals? Select yes or no.

	Yes	No
Circle		
Star		
Square		
Rectangle		

17. Circle the parallelogram.

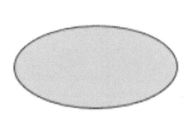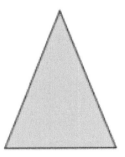

18. For each polygon in the first column, an attribute is defined in the second column. Write true, if the polygon has the mentioned attribute or write false if the polygon does not have the mentioned attribute.

Polygon	Attribute	True or False
Rhombus	It has two sets of parallel sides	True
Parallelogram	All the angles are equal	
Rectangle	Opposite sides are equal	

19. Draw a quadrilateral which has three obtuse angles.
    Instruction : An obtuse angle is an angle which measures more than 90° but less than 180°.

20. Which of the following figures have at least one set parallel sides? Note that more than one option may be correct.

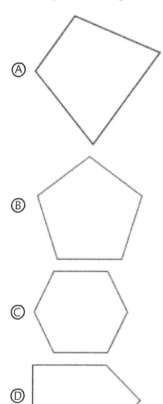

Ⓐ

Ⓑ

Ⓒ

Ⓓ

Chapter 6

Lesson 2: Shape Partitions

You can scan the QR code given below or use the url to access additional EdSearch resources including videos and mobile apps related to *Shape Partitions*.

ed)Search **Shape Partitions**	
URL	**QR Code**
http://www.lumoslearning.com/a/3ga2	

1. What is the dotted line that divides a shape into two equal parts called?

    Ⓐ a middle line
    Ⓑ a line of symmetry
    Ⓒ a line of congruency
    Ⓓ a divider

2. A square has how many lines of symmetry?

    Ⓐ 8
    Ⓑ 4
    Ⓒ 1
    Ⓓ 2

3. Which of the following has NO lines of symmetry?

    Ⓐ

    Ⓑ

    Ⓒ

    Ⓓ

4. Which of the following objects has more than one line of symmetry?

Ⓐ

Ⓑ

Ⓒ

Ⓓ

5. What fraction of this triangle is shaded?

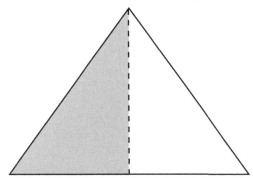

Ⓐ $\frac{1}{2}$

Ⓑ $\frac{2}{2}$

Ⓒ $\frac{0}{2}$

Ⓓ $\frac{3}{4}$

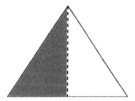
6. **What fraction of this triangle is shaded?**

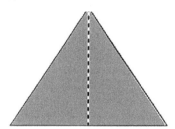

(A) $\dfrac{0}{2}$

(B) $\dfrac{1}{2}$

(C) $\dfrac{2}{2}$

(D) $\dfrac{3}{4}$

7. **What fraction of this triangle is shaded?**

(A) $\dfrac{0}{2}$

(B) $\dfrac{1}{2}$

(C) $\dfrac{2}{2}$

(D) $\dfrac{3}{4}$

8. **What fraction of this square is shaded?**

Ⓐ $\dfrac{0}{2}$

Ⓑ $\dfrac{1}{2}$

Ⓒ $\dfrac{2}{2}$

Ⓓ $\dfrac{3}{4}$

9. **What fraction of this square is shaded?**

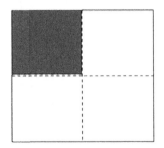

Ⓐ $\dfrac{0}{4}$

Ⓑ $\dfrac{1}{4}$

Ⓒ $\dfrac{2}{4}$

Ⓓ $\dfrac{1}{2}$

10. What fraction of this square is shaded?

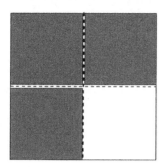

Ⓐ $\dfrac{0}{4}$

Ⓑ $\dfrac{1}{4}$

Ⓒ $\dfrac{1}{2}$

Ⓓ $\dfrac{3}{4}$

11. What fraction of this rectangle is shaded?

Ⓐ $\dfrac{0}{4}$

Ⓑ $\dfrac{1}{4}$

Ⓒ $\dfrac{2}{4}$

Ⓓ $\dfrac{3}{4}$

12. What fraction of this circle is shaded?

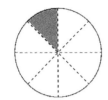

Ⓐ $\dfrac{1}{8}$

Ⓑ $\dfrac{1}{4}$

Ⓒ $\dfrac{1}{2}$

Ⓓ $\dfrac{3}{4}$

13. What fraction of this circle is shaded?

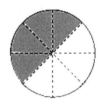

Ⓐ $\dfrac{1}{8}$

Ⓑ $\dfrac{1}{4}$

Ⓒ $\dfrac{5}{8}$

Ⓓ $\dfrac{4}{8}$

14. The area of the entire rectangle shown below is 48 square feet. What is the area of the shaded portion?

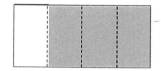

Ⓐ 36 square feet
Ⓑ 48 square feet
Ⓒ 144 square feet
Ⓓ 12 square feet

15. If the area of the entire rectangle below is 36 square feet. What is the area of the shaded portion?

Ⓐ 8 square feet
Ⓑ 9 square feet
Ⓒ 144 square feet
Ⓓ 12 square feet

16. Do these figures have a line of symmetry? Select yes or no.

	Yes	No

17. Circle the shape that has a line of symmetry.

18. If the area of the whole rectangle is 28, what is the area of the shaded portion? Write your answer in the box given below.

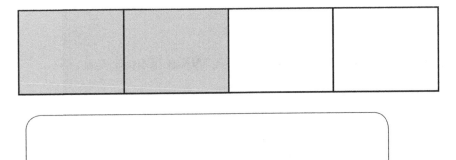

19. Shade one third of the figure below.

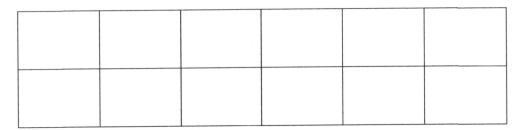

20. A circle has an area of 96 sq. cm. The circle is divided into 8 equal parts. Which of the following statements are correct? Select all the correct answers.

   Ⓐ If you shade 3 parts, the area of the shaded portion is 32 sq. cm.
   Ⓑ If you shade 4 parts, the area of the shaded portion is 48 sq. cm.
   Ⓒ If you shade 7 parts, the area of the shaded portion is 84 sq. cm.
   Ⓓ If you shade 2 parts, the area of the shaded portion is 24 sq. cm.

End of Geometry

GMAS FAQs

What will GMAS Assessment Look Like?

In many ways, the GMAS assessments will be unlike anything many students have ever seen. The tests will be conducted online, requiring students complete tasks to assess a deeper understanding of the Georgia standards. The students will take the Summative Assessment at the end of the year.

The time for the Math Summative assessment for each grade is given below:

Estimated Time on Task in Minutes		
Grade	Section 1	Section 2
3	65	65
4	65	65
5	65	65
6	65	65
7	65	65
8	65	65

How is this Lumos tedBook aligned to GMAS Guidelines?

The practice tests provided in the Lumos Program were created to reflect the depth and rigor of the GMAS assessments based on the information published by the test administrator. However, the content and format of the GMAS assessment that is officially administered to the students could be different compared to these practice tests. You can get more information about this test by visiting https://www.gadoe.org/Curriculum-Instruction-and-Assessment/Assessment/Pages/EOG-Study-Resource-Guides.aspx

What item types are included in the Online GMAS Test?

Because the assessment is online, the test will consist of a combination of new types of questions:

1. Selected Response or Multiple choice questions
2. Multi select or two part questions
3. Drag and Drop
4. Hot text
5. Equation editor
6. Plot the point
7. Bar chart

For more information on 2021-22 Assessment year, visit

http://www.lumoslearning.com/a/gmas-2021-faqs

OR Scan the **QR Code**

Discover Engaging and Relevant Learning Resources

Lumos EdSearch is a safe search engine specifically designed for teachers and students. Using EdSearch, you can easily find thousands of standards-aligned learning resources such as questions, videos, lessons, worksheets and apps. Teachers can use EdSearch to create custom resource kits to perfectly match their lesson objective and assign them to one or more students in their classroom.

To access the EdSearch tool, use the search box after you log into Lumos StepUp or use the link provided below.

http://www.lumoslearning.com/a/edsearchb	

The Lumos Standards Coherence map provides information about previous level, next level and related standards. It helps educators and students visually explore learning standards. It's an effective tool to help students progress through the learning objectives. Teachers can use this tool to develop their own pacing charts and lesson plans. Educators can also use the coherence map to get deep insights into why a student is struggling in a specific learning objective.

Teachers can access the Coherence maps after logging into the StepUp Teacher Portal or use the link provided below.

http://www.lumoslearning.com/a/coherence-map	

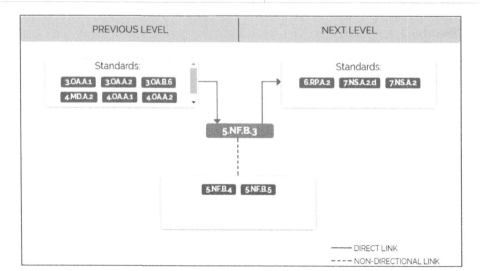

What if I buy more than one Lumos Study Program?

Step 1

Visit the URL and login to your account.
http://www.lumoslearning.com

Step 2

Click on 'My tedBooks' under the "Account" tab.
Place the Book Access Code and submit.

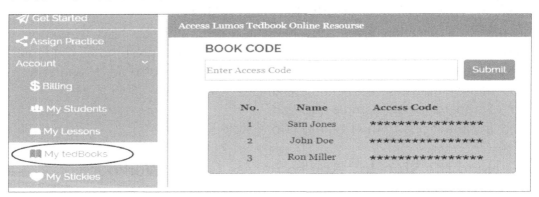

Step 3

To add the new book for a registered student, choose the
○ Existing Student button and select the student and submit.

Assign To ⊕

⦿ Existing Student   ○ Add New student

○ Sam Jones

○ John Doe

○ Ron Miller

Submit

To add the new book for a new student, choose the ○ Add New student
button and complete the student registration.

Assign To ⊕

○ Existing Student   ⦿ Add New student

Register Your TedBook

Student Name:*   Enter First Name   Enter Last Name

Student Login*

Password*

Submit

Lumos StepUp® Mobile App FAQ For Students

What is the Lumos StepUp® App?

It is a FREE application you can download onto your Android Smartphones, tablets, iPhones, and iPads.

What are the Benefits of the StepUp® App?

This mobile application gives convenient access to Practice Tests, Common Core State Standards, Online Workbooks, and learning resources through your Smartphone and tablet computers.

- Fourteen Technology enhanced question types in both MATH and ELA
- Sample questions for Arithmetic drills
- Standard specific sample questions
- Instant access to the Common Core State Standards

Do I Need the StepUp® App to Access Online Workbooks?

No, you can access Lumos StepUp® Online Workbooks through a personal computer. The StepUp® app simply enhances your learning experience and allows you to conveniently access StepUp® Online Workbooks and additional resources through your smart phone or tablet.

How can I Download the App?

Visit **lumoslearning.com/a/stepup-app** using your Smartphone or tablet and follow the instructions to download the app.

**QR Code
for Smartphone
Or Tablet Users**

Lumos StepUp® Mobile App FAQ
For Parents and Teachers

What is the Lumos StepUp® App?

It is a free app that teachers can use to easily access real-time student activity information as well as assign learning resources to students. Parents can also use it to easily access school-related information such as homework assigned by teachers and PTA meetings. It can be downloaded onto smart phones and tablets from popular App Stores.

What are the Benefits of the Lumos StepUp® App?

It provides convenient access to

- Standards aligned learning resources for your students
- An easy to use Dashboard
- Student progress reports
- Active and inactive students in your classroom
- Professional development information
- Educational Blogs

How can I Download the App?

Visit **lumoslearning.com/a/stepup-app** using your Smartphone or tablet and follow the instructions to download the app.

**QR Code
for Smartphone
Or Tablet Users**

Progress Chart

Standard		Lesson	Page No.	Practice		Mastered	Re-practice /Reteach
GMAS	**CCSS**			Date	Score		
MGSE3.OA.1	3.OA.A.1	Understanding Multiplication	10				
MGSE3.OA.2	3.OA.A.2	Understanding Division	19				
MGSE3.OA.3	3.OA.A.3	Applying Multiplication & Division	25				
MGSE3.OA.4	3.OA.A.4	Finding Unknown Values	31				
MGSE3.OA.5	3.OA.B.5	Multiplication & Division Properties	37				
MGSE3.OA.6	3.OA.B.6	Relating Multiplication & Division	43				
MGSE3.OA.7	3.OA.C.7	Multiplication & Division Facts	49				
MGSE3.OA.8	3.OA.D.8	Two-Step Problems	57				
MGSE3.OA.9	3.OA.D.9	Number Patterns	63				
MGSE3.NBT.1	3.NBT.A.1	Rounding Numbers	69				
MGSE3.NBT.2	3.NBT.A.2	Addition & Subtraction	74				
MGSE3.NBT.3	3.NBT.A.3	Multiplying Multiples of 10	79				
MGSE3.NF.1	3.NF.A.1	Fractions of a Whole	85				
MGSE3.NF.2	3.NF.A.2	Fractions on the Number Line	93				
MGSE3.NF.3	3.NF.A.3	Comparing Fractions	101				

Standard		Lesson	Page No.	Practice		Mastered	Re-practice /Reteach
GMAS	CCSS			Date	Score		
MGSE3.MD.1	3.MD.A.1	Telling Time	108				
MGSE3.MD.1	3.MD.A.1	Elapsed Time	115				
MGSE3.MD.2	3.MD.A.2	Liquid Volume & Mass	121				
MGSE3.MD.3	3.MD.B.3	Graphs	126				
MGSE3.MD.4	3.MD.B.4	Measuring Length	138				
MGSE3.MD.6	3.MD.C.6	Area	143				
MGSE3.MD.7	3.MD.C.7	Relating Area to Addition & Multiplication	149				
MGSE3.MD.8	3.MD.D.8	Perimeter	154				
MGSE3.G.1	3.G.A.1	2-Dimensional Shapes	164				
MGSE3.G.2	3.G.A.2	Shape Partitions	170				

Lumos Learning
Developed by Expert Teachers

Grade **3**

GEORGIA
ENGLISH
LANGUAGE ARTS LITERACY
GMAS Practice

Student Copy

Updated for 2021-22

(((**tedBook**)))

ONLINE

2 GMAS Practice Tests
7 Question Types

Available

- At Leading book stores
- Online www.LumosLearning.com